Other Books by Adin Steinsaltz

The Essential Talmud
In the Beginning
The Long Shorter Way
The Strife of the Spirit
The Sustaining Utterance
The Tales of Rabbi Nachman of Bratslav
The Thirteen Petalled Rose

Biblical Images

Biblical Images

Adin Steinsaltz

*Translated by Yehuda Hanegbi
and Yehudit Keshet*

JASON ARONSON INC.
*Northvale, New Jersey
London*

Chapter 1 was translated by Michael Swirsky.

This book was set in 13pt. Berkeley Oldstyle by Alpha Graphics of Pittsfield, New Hampshire, and printed by Haddon Craftsmen in Scranton, Pennsylvania.

Copyright © 1994, 1984, by Adin Steinsaltz

10 9 8 7 6 5 4 3 2

Library of Congress Cataloging-in-Publication Data

Steinsaltz, Adin.
    Biblical images / Adin Steinsaltz ; translated by Yehuda Hanegbi and Yehudit Keshet. — [Enl. ed.]
      p. cm.
    "Chapter 1 was translated by Michael Swirsky"—Prelim. matter.
    Includes index.
    ISBN 1-56821-178-3
    1. Bible. O.T.—Biography. I. Title.
    BS571.S82 1994
    221.9'22—dc20
    [B]   94-579

Manufactured in the United States of America. Jason Aronson Inc. offers books and cassettes. For information and catalog write to Jason Aronson Inc., 230 Livingston Street, Northvale, New Jersey 07647.

For the respect of my parents,
Miriam and Alfred Goldschlager,
who made it possible for me to dedicate this book;

In loving memory
of the many generations
of our Jewish people whom we follow,
and especially my wife Dina's forefather
Rabbi Moshe Ben Maimon (the Rambam);

And for our children and the future generations,
who form the continuity of our people
due to the inspiration and education of great teachers
whom we are privileged to be touched by,
such as our very dear Rabbi Adin Steinsaltz—
May HaShem grant him good health
to continue his great work.

Ron Goldschlager
Melbourne, Australia

Contents

v

CONTENTS

Acknowledgments

This book is the product of two series of lectures that were first broadcast over Galei Tzahal, the army channel of Israel Radio, and were subsequently published in book form by the Ministry of Defence, Tel Aviv: *Sketches of Bible Personalities* (1981); *Women in the Bible* (1983). I would like to thank Tirzah Yuval-Elhanati, producer of the series, for initiating these broadcasts.

A further opportunity to prepare and edit this material in more final form came while I was the guest of the Institute for Advanced Studies at Princeton during 1982, and I wish to express my gratitude to Dr. Harry Woolf, Director of the Institute, for making this opportunity possible.

Special thanks are also due to my friend, Dr. Leon Canick, for his support and encouragement during the final stages of this work.

Warm gratitude is certainly due to Milton

Taubman for providing the means for preparing this translation and others. Finally, my thanks to the translators of the book who labored lovingly to turn the complex text, with its subtle hints and allusions, into readable English: Yehuda Hanegbi, for the chapters on the men of the Bible; Yehudit Keshet, for those on the women; and Michael Swirsky, for the chapter on Eve.

Introduction

The characters and heroes of the Bible are without doubt some of the best-known figures in history. Even people who are not well versed in the Scriptures, and who do not read the Bible regularly, know at least the names of some of the major personalities. We encounter them again and again, directly or indirectly, in art, in literature, in speech, or in folklore. And yet these biblical men and women remain among the most elusive, enigmatic, and least understood of any heroes. This lack of knowledge and understanding is not necessarily a function of ignorance but stems rather from the fact that the biblical personae are so familiar, so "famous," that they have become almost stereotyped. They have fallen victim to accepted patterns of thinking, been fitted into conventional molds and subjected to unquestioning assumptions that have prevented any attempt at deeper understanding. It is not uncommon for the very thing that "everyone knows" not to receive the attention it deserves.

However, there is another, more crucial, factor at work here, and that is the nature of the biblical narrative itself, which confronts even those thoroughly familiar with an actual story with a bewildering blankness regarding the personalities portrayed in it.

Two fundamental elements in the Scriptures lend these accounts their special character and power and produce the mystery surrounding the protagonists. Scriptural style is almost always objective and distant; the heroes and heroines are not idealized but are seen, as it were, from above, in a way that is both more comprehensive and, at the same time, more detached than the standard historical chronicle. The narrative is also as factual as possible, with no attempt to penetrate the psyche of the characters or to analyze their motives. The techniques and tricks of dramatists, the revealing monologue, the intimate conversation to explain dreams and longings, a chorus providing background details are all absent in the Scriptures. It is this almost dry style that gives the biblical story its impact. Here, every sentence, every action counts, indicating by means of the most subtle allusions occurrences whose significance resounds in the souls of men and in the world at large. We see the events, but their implications remain obscure; we see the outcome of the events, without ever knowing clearly anything of their internal mechanisms. What did Abraham think as he led his son Isaac to the sacrifice? How did Moses feel when the Almighty revealed Himself? Why did Absalom rebel against his father? We can only guess at the answers to these questions: in the Scriptures, no word is said about them.

Another aspect of this detached view is the multifaceted picture it provides. Although the distinction between good and evil, between sinners and saints is clearcut and unequivocal, there is no attempt to adjust events and incidents to suit the general image of a personality. The great men and women who serve as examples and models for all generations are not described only in terms of glowing admiration. Their failings, failures, and difficulties are described with the same objectivity as are those of the sinful; and the contrary is also true: the good points of those generally considered to be negative personalities are also shown. The "good guys" of the Scriptures are not plaster saints, all "sweetness and light"; nor are the "bad guys" monsters, but human beings shown in all their many (and sometimes contradictory) aspects.

The biblical persona is shown not only in his or her true colors but also in the context of a wider dimension. One's worth as an individual is never judged simply on the basis of one's private existence, but also in terms of broad implications. Biblical heroes and heroines have their private lives, but their every action has, too, a significance for society at large. The private life of a given figure may be a model of goodness and decency (at least in his or her own eyes) but may well be quite destructive in terms of society. On the other hand, the private sin may not always lead to a negative outcome in the context of family, society, or state. In the Bible, events are measured in relation not only to the time in which they occur, but also to the whole spectrum of historical time, which inevitably leads to changes in the evaluation of deeds and events and in the relationship between great and small, between the important and the trivial. Thus, the great and powerful ruler turns out to be a small and insignificant historical episode, and the persecuted wretch proves to be the only significant person in a whole era.

This yardstick of significance extends beyond the judgment of history, because in the Scriptures all these are measured in terms not only of finite time but also of eternity. Yet no matter how exalted its viewpoint, the general judgment of events and people, the Bible relates to all dimensions—the exalted and the abstract alongside the petty details of life as it is lived at the mundane, human level. The exaltation here can also encompass the transient, the minor, the passing dream. Thus, the biblical narrative is built on sweeping generalizations encompassing large periods of time and fascinating events at the same time as it relates to the smallest of precise details. The greatest in the world is not described as greater than the ability of man to relate to; and the smallest is never too trivial, but always important for the understanding of existence.

The bold strokes of the biblical canvas are supplemented here and there by highly detailed miniatures; and together these images produce remarkable, multidimensional portraits, full of life and vigor. It is these characteristics that produce the beauty and power of the biblical story and also lead to the difficulty of understanding the characters. No story is simple and one-dimensional; no character self-explanatory. As in real life, there are variations and contradictions; and, as in real life, they hint at solutions without actually providing them.

There is another aspect to the problem of biblical personae. The Bible is not a book to be idly read in passing, and the men and women of the Scriptures are more than mere life portraits: they continue to live and function long after their deaths in this world. The ancient Jewish custom of speaking of biblical characters in the present tense is an expression of a genuine experience. These are not ordinary historical figures but archetypes; as such, their lives are carried on and continue not only in literature and philosophy but in the lives of their descendents throughout the generations. In a sense, they continue to live and also to evolve throughout Jewish history, in its psychic experience, and as part of the collective personality of the Jewish nation.

The extensive midrashic literature, together with the innumerable commentaries that have been produced over the generations, have filled in dimensions and aspects of the biblical personalities only hinted at in Scripture itself. No biblical story is complete without these additional strata of content, which add new forms and lines to each portrait, solving some problems, adding new material, and producing new outlines that in turn must be filled in and completed.

This collection of selected portraits of biblical characters is an attempt to fill in some of the outlines in the picture, to clarify certain things hinted at in the Scriptures. It is an attempt to understand some well-known biblical figures from within, to analyze their motives, and to try to understand their spiritual experiences and aspirations in the context of the historical period in which they lived. In order to try to present a complete picture and not merely to be content with historical hindsight, this material is drawn from traditional Jewish sources. In most cases, these sources are not listed, since the material is culled from many levels and types of the rich treasury of Jewish literature; and, in the nature of things, much more is alluded to than is explicitly written. Readers who are familiar with these sources will be able to recognize the allusions to a greater or lesser degree, while those who are outside the world of Jewish scholarship would merely be confused by detailed references.

Because of the complexity of the Bible personae, it has not been possible to discuss them in all their various aspects. These chapters are therefore intended as a commentary on one facet of a given character—a viewpoint that illuminates him or her in a certain way and is also relevant to the problems and events of the present day.

The need to deal with a limited canvas naturally reduces the scope of each portrait, so that each chapter should be seen as the elaboration and perfection of one detail within the whole. Thus, certain personalities have been omitted because this framework would make it impossible to do justice to their overall importance. Jacob, Moses, and David are such fundamental, multidimensional characters that it would be inappropriate to restrict oneself to one or the other side of their personalities.

The personages in this book have therefore a dual significance. They are biblical-historical characters and also archetypal figures in some way relevant to the inner life of the modern individual, and to modern society and politics as well. Not all these people were model characters; they include the good and the bad, those whose acts we perpetuate today and those who have served as a warning and a deterrent to repeating the mistakes of the past.

Most of all, this book is not intended to provide all the answers, but rather to encourage the reader to become better acquainted with the men and women of the Bible, to read—or reread—the Scriptures for himself or herself and to rediscover the pleasure of studying the Bible: for it is a map through the past, a guide for the present, and a directory to the future.

1

Eve

THE MISSING HALF

ve is not merely the first woman to be mentioned in the Scriptures; she is the first woman. Thus, even more than other biblical figures, she is an archetype, the mother and precursor of women in general. In a sense, every man, at some stage in his life, is Adam, and every woman is Eve. The Adam-Eve relationship is fundamental to every life pattern. We come back again and again, in a multiplicity of guises and forms, to these two prototypes, for Adam and Eve represent the complete course of human life: in other words, they project an image not of men in their individuality and particularity, but of man as a species, of humanity as humanity. So it is that the mystics

---

The story of Eve is to be found in Genesis 2:18-4:2. Similar references will denote the source of succeeding chapters.

taught that all human souls are not only descended from Adam but are actually dependent upon him, are components of his being. Adam is that man who includes all men. Adam and Eve are not merely archetypes but the very stuff of mankind, and their story is the story of the human race.

Such an interpretation of the story of Eve opens the way to a comprehensive view of women, for, as I have implied, every woman is part of Eve at one time or another and in some way or another plays Eve's role over and over again. This is not to say that Eve is necessarily to be held up as a model. Not even the most exemplary female figures in Jewish history are without flaw. The four matriarchs themselves—Sarah, Rebekah, Leah, and Rachel—who are in many respects the paragons of Jewish womanhood, have not been immune to criticism by the talmudic sages or by the leading lights of other generations either. Indeed, none of the great biblical personalities comes across as an unambiguous or one-dimensional embodiment of sweetness and light. All are real, live people with their triumphs and failures, strengths and temptations, inhibitions and struggles. At times, it is an individual's very failing or flaw that is intended to be instructive. All these personalities in the Bible are, in some sense, object lessons, although they are not necessarily to be imitated. On the contrary, the purpose of a given narrative is often to warn us against the mistakes of our ancestors, however great and important and even superior to us the latter may have been. Thus, for example, Eve's story is the story of a woman, with all a woman's grace and beauty, on the one hand, and all her capacity to corrupt and be corrupted, on the other. Eve is both a positive example and a warning concerning female power and the female role in the world.

The story of Adam and Eve is multifaceted, and I shall touch on only a few aspects of it. The first thing that is important to understand about Eve is the seemingly simple matter of her creation, which, in turn, reflects a certain notion of her relationship to Adam. The talmudic sages agreed that Eve was not simply born from Adam's rib, as we are somehow accustomed to think, but that Adam and Eve (or rather *ha-adam ha-rishon*, "primordial man") came into being as a single creature with two faces or sides—the one, male; the other, female. The biblical word *tsela*, usually understood to mean "rib," could be taken in the sense of "side" as in the phrase *tsela'ot hamishkan* ("the sides of the Sanctuary"). Woman was created from Adam's *tsela* because she was to begin with a *tsela*, or a side or aspect of primordial man, who thus came to be two distinct persons.

This notion is reinforced when one looks beyond the story of the creation of man, to its implications as they are spelled out in what follows. The idea of creation as separation recurs both in the

Scriptures themselves and, afterward, throughout Jewish literature. Hence, the upshot is that the relationship between men and women in all times and places has the character of the quest for something lost, to use the talmudic expression. Male and female are essentially parts of a single whole, originally created as one being; but for various reasons—principally the establishment of a different, more complex, and perhaps deeper kind of connection between the two—the whole body is divided. The two half bodies are constantly in search of one another and find no fulfillment until they are rejoined, in a new and different unity. The words of Scripture that follow—"Therefore shall a man leave his father and his mother, and shall cleave unto his wife: and they shall be one flesh" (Genesis 2:24)—relate primarily to the event of the division. The implication is that, while the filial tie is very strong—indeed, virtually unbreakable—there is another tie, hidden, but nonetheless present at birth: the tie with a future partner.

This tie is even more fundamental to the child's being than the tie with his parents, so that he eventually abandons them and goes in search of his lost "better half." His quest is for his own completeness, for the wholeness of his own flesh that he lost when, in the second creation, he was divided, as it were, into two. What he seeks is a return to his primordial oneness.

According to this view, the male–female relationship was originally intended not as a means of procreation but rather as something more basic and primary. Procreation is a secondary function: in the story of the Creation and of Eve, childbirth makes its appearance later, as a surprising new dimension to the relationship between men and women. In a sense, the birth of a child is a kind of bonus, a new creation, a new man, wondrously brought into being by the very act of reunification. The primordial oneness in itself appeared to be sterile; but, in recovering that oneness, the two uniting parts create out of themselves something that has had no earlier existence. And, indeed, the narrative describing the first childbirth and the first children emphasizes the marvel of this new creation, this new world. The basic male-female tie is not a function but an essential bond, the reunification of two essences. As a consequence, the family, too, comes to be seen as being part of the primal essence of man and not merely as a social device for meeting one need or another.

The story of the separation, of the halving of the original human personality, sheds light on a basic difference between man and other living creatures. The latter are from the outset created as male and female. Hence, the relationship between the two sexes is, in their case, based upon the task of reproduction rather than on any inherent meaning in the relationship. To borrow a phrase from the medieval sage Rabbi Moshe ben

Nachman, "No bull takes a cow to wife." The bond is accidental, opportunistic, and functional in a way in which the human conjugal tie cannot be.

It thus becomes clear that the story of the creation of Eve from the *tsela* is more than just an incidental account; it is essential to an understanding of human marital and familial ties and to the whole elaboration, later, of ways of strengthening them. The great body of Jewish marital law and custom in all its detail is basically an extension and formalization of the original role of the first woman, Eve. The sanctity of marriage, the laws that govern marital relations, the prohibitions against adultery and incest, the broad conceptual framework governing marital relations–indeed, all relations between the sexes–are all outgrowths of the basic conception of Eve as having been severed from Adam. To this very day, a nuptial blessing–"May You cause the bride and groom to rejoice as You did Your creation in the primeval Garden of Eden"–reminds us of this motif. In effect, every wedding is a return to the primordial state of Adam and Eve.

Another important element in the Eden story is the role of Eve as arch-temptress and hence the one responsible for the expulsion from the Garden. The description of Eve's seduction by the serpent and her seduction of Adam raises many questions that have troubled students in every age–among them the question why this particular sequence of events and why it was Eve who tempted Adam.

One of the significant explanations turns upon a peculiarity of this first human generation that was afterward rectified. Adam, it seems, had been commanded directly by God, while Eve received the commandment only through Adam. From this circumstance, a far-reaching conclusion can be drawn: obedience to the divine imperative, whether negative or positive, must be based upon a direct personal relationship. When, in the absence of such a relationship, obligation is mediated through some third party, failure is invited. The story of the theophany at Sinai, which in its inward form, describing the "creation" of Israel, recapitulates the story of Adam's creation, is essentially a reversal of the expulsion from Eden. Here the commandments are given quite differently: the whole house of Israel, men and women alike, step forth to receive the Torah together. The *Rishonim* (medieval rabbinic commentators) even find hints that the Torah had to be accepted *first* by the women (the "house of Jacob") before it could be accepted by the men (the "house of Israel"). There is thus a rectification of the original pattern, based— at least in part—on the need for directness in a true relationship.

There are other explanations as well that, at the very least, provide food for thought. A problem that engaged the sages of the Talmud in a variety of ways was what they called "the added measure of understanding given to women"—women's intuition—which implied, among other things, that they have an extra degree of curiosity. The incident of the Tree of Knowledge turns, after all, partly on the arousal of curiosity, the temptation to know too much. Curiosity is not in itself considered to be bad or conducive to sin, but inquiry beyond permissible limits is always dangerous and sometimes corrupting. Hence, the attempt to set a variety of limitations upon women's inquisitiveness.

From another point of view, also much discussed, the sin of the Tree of Knowledge is connected to the special character of the male-female relationship. The subject of this sin is, of course, very broad and includes within its purview questions of knowledge versus innocence, life, and death.

Human beings are the only living creatures whose sex lives are not circumscribed by a reproductive code. We are indeed emancipated to a unique degree from the cycle of nature; it is conscious relatedness and emotion that are decisive for us, not biological instinct, which serves merely as an underpinning.

The question of knowledge (*da'at*) in this context and certainly of the Tree of Knowledge must be seen in the light of the use of the same Hebrew root to describe the relationship of the first human beings to each other: "And Adam knew (*yada'*) Eve his wife" (Genesis 4:1). The Tree of Knowledge thus represents not so much the loss of the primal innocence of Eden, but rather the loss of one set of relationships and their replacement by another, quite different set. Instead of the sort of practical, instrumental male-female connection that prevails in the rest of nature, we have the advantage of a tie that is largely free of stubborn biological determination. On the other hand, this very freedom gives rise to the evil impulse, a wild desire that knows no inherent bounds or limitations, including its own original function. Other human instincts—hunger, thirst—are clearly related to specific functional ends and reach satiation when those ends are achieved; the sex drive appears to have no aim other than its own gratification. It is thus distinctively human desire, with its unique potential for achieving intimacy as well as for wanton aggrandizement, that the Tree of Knowledge introduces into the world.

The existence of sexual prohibitions in every culture reflects the universal sense of the strangeness of this distinctively human pattern; and thus the sin of the Tree of Knowledge is described as stemming, not from hunger or thirst, but from a "lusting of the eyes," an attraction to the beauty of the fruit as an end in itself. It is pure desire, with no utilitarian purpose. The appearance of such desire is specifically linked with the woman, for whereas in all other species reproduction depends upon the susceptibility of the female, much more than the male, to a cycle of sexual readiness, in the human female alone such a cycle (as distinct from the reproductive cycle *per se*) no longer exists, and sexual activity is a constant possibility. The sin of the Tree of Knowledge thus begins with the woman, for it is she who reveals in her own makeup the possibility of emancipation from the cyclical, mechanical workings of instinct. Had man remained within the bonds of instinct, of urges built into his own biology, he might have remained in the Garden of Eden in a world of much beauty and contentment but also of limitation. Through the Tree of Knowledge, a new world came into being with the free play of desire. There emerged also freedom of choice. The sin of the Tree of Knowledge is both the first sin and the key to this new world. Only after many generations, after thousands of years, can the human race, in the fullness of its freedom, attempt to reconstruct for itself functional frameworks that might belatedly rectify the first sin, give it positive meaning, and thus annul it *qua* sin, turning it rather into a purpose and a task.

2

Abraham

THE RENOVATOR

braham is the hero of an epos that is peculiar to Israel and stands out with a greatness of its own in the history of mankind.

The Bible story tells us a great deal about the man and his ideas, the way he lived, his friends and enemies, his family, and so on. Having been told so much, the question may well be asked: What, after all, did he do? What makes him a central figure in the memory of the race? Key figures in history are not ordinary persons, and we usually attach some descriptive epithet to a great name: a noble conqueror, an artistic genius, an intrepid explorer, the founder of an empire, and so on. How can we define the greatness of Abraham?

Genesis 12:1–22:19.

The most accepted answer to this question—throughout the generations—has been the view that Abraham was the innovator of monotheism: that he gave us the faith in one God. He is alleged to have been the first to conceive and develop the idea, and thereby to have founded the Jewish people and all the monotheistic religions and, consequently, much of the philosophy and modes of thought that lie at the source of our civilization.

Nevertheless, despite the vivid *Midrash* of the young Abram smashing the idols, this view of the father of the nation as principally an iconoclast is not accepted by serious scholars. A rereading of the Bible text is enough to show that there is no mention of Abraham's role as a great prophet bringing to the world the belief in a single God. Many wonderful things are related about the man, and his stature holds up to any critical scrutiny. His deeds and character are in fact recollected with love and reverence in many tales, with descriptions of his faith and devotion, his wanderings, his courage, his hospitality, and even his weaknesses. But the fact that he was the originator of monotheism is not mentioned.

In point of fact, a closer examination of the Genesis story and of the many exegeses leads to a different view of the man and sheds light on many other developments in religious history. To begin with, according to the Bible itself, the belief in one God is not anything new, nor is it the peak of some evolutionary development. Monotheism is not a higher stage of some process of growth following on a lower stage of polytheism. Monotheism is itself primary and basic; it has been the dominant mode of worship from as far back as human memory goes. All the other modes of religious faith came after it, and not before. For this truth, the scriptural text itself, though it does not say so in precisely this fashion, is the chief evidence. And like Maimonides and other Jewish sages, modern scholarship, especially in the field of anthropology, tends to question whether polytheism, even in its primitive forms such as fetishism or voodoo, is not a degeneration of primary monotheistic cults.

In other words, even the most primitive of peoples evince a faith in a higher power. It may be stretching the point to call this monotheism in the modern sense of the term, because the primitive mentality cannot make abstractions to the same degree. Nevertheless, a basic belief in one supreme basic power that makes everything happen in the universe is common to all—even to the bushmen of Africa or the inhabitants of the Tierra del Fuego in South America, peoples thoroughly isolated from other cultural influences. Their fundamental belief is not in many gods or even in various forces of nature that have to be propitiated; it is a belief in or worship of one power, one essence or thing that takes on the dimensions of the utmost

grandeur their psyche can conceive. This fundamental stance of the human before the holy, which
is just within and yet beyond conception, is not
necessarily a matter of man's relation to any specific force of nature, or to a person or awesome
image, or even to gods and demons. It is the primary sensation of "little me," which is the true
feeling of every human being when facing the
mysterious beyond.

This is the genesis point in the soul. From it two
different courses may be taken. One may hold fast
to this primal unity against the impact of the inexplicable and bear up to all that such a position
implies. This course would lead to a faith in a
single God. The alternative development would
be from the unity to the multiplicity. In other
words, from simple monotheism—the direct faith
in something not specific or clearly oriented
(which is perhaps like the faith of a child)—to a
complex faith, derived from the endeavor to iso-
late certain things and subjects. At first, there is
the concept of the whole, because man cannot yet
define any specific force or thing. Afterward, the
whole begins to be analyzed, broken down into
parts and categories: fire, water, air, earth, sun, and
the like. Feelings of fear, gratitude, and shame lead
to rites of worship of that eminent force of nature
that seems to be most endowed with a life and
consciousness of its own. In turn, it itself becomes
a complex and variegated system of forces, each

with a character of its own and ultimately with a representative god of its own.

After further development and degeneration, the stage is reached of the image or figure. The graven image is not the father of the god but its offspring. At first, the image is the symbol of the Divine's power; but, after a certain decline of the power of faith, men no longer present themselves before the primal force or the symbol but relate to the physical image, the statue. Then follows the worship of these statues and pictures and of whatever else is given to visual perception, touch, caress.

Idolatry of this sort is, therefore, not the first or the most primitive stage of religion. It is a later development in a certain direction. It is a transition from the primal belief in an unknown God to a worship of tangible and comprehensible gods. The great amalgam of the infinite is very difficult to negotiate with. It is much easier to relate to some specific force or image and to propitiate "him" with offerings and to expect certain responses in the way of rewards and punishments.

Polytheism is thus a complicated and sophisticated system of worship springing from the need to establish a "rational" and direct contact with the Divine. Instead of trying to communicate with a basic supreme essence, polytheism believes in the possibility of usefulness of intermediaries, such as specific gods or a set of semidivine forces.

Even the Hindu scriptures (like those of most other "polytheistic" religions) recognize the existence of a supreme formless Divine, the Atman, who cannot be reached by man except through the functional gods—which increase in number the nearer they get to the popular mind. And, of course, this is the perspective of the Bible itself. The first man is seen as a whole, the archetype of a direct relation with a single hidden God. The following generations "began to call on the name of God" (Genesis 4:26), and this, according to a certain exegesis, indicated that men were beginning to attach significance to other forces—of nature, symbols, and images, whether genuine or false. A system of well-defined forces that provide a reasonable explanation for things is the product of an advanced culture, with a philosophy, science, astronomy, and so on.

This intellectual world of polytheistic religion—with all its sophistication and corruption—was the world in which the patriarch Abraham lived. He did not emerge from a pastoral world of wandering shepherds, uncouth and unlearned. He came from great cities, centers of culture and hubs of commerce. In these cities, there were banks and letters of credit, as in our own day, even if documents were written on bricks of clay. A world of elaborate civilization, already ancient and worldly-wise in its own way: Ur of the Chaldees, Babylon, Egypt. . . . It was a polytheistic, idolatrous urbanity, the height of an ancient culture, representing the most advanced ideas and the most refined concepts in science, art, and philosophy.

And in this world, the "modern" world of the ancient past, Abraham found himself believing in a single God. It was not a new discovery on his part; on the contrary, it was a reaffirmation of a very old truth, one that had almost been forgotten and was probably considered by his contemporaries as barbaric and primitive. Abraham was thus not an innovator but an ultraconservative, like someone belonging to a cult of ancient origin. On the other hand, Abraham did represent something very new: he was a prophet in that he called for a renewal of faith, a return (almost a repentance) to the divine Oneness. He tried to restore the faith of a distant past; but his contemporaries probably saw him as a crude and rather old-fashioned preacher.

One of the proofs offered by the Bible itself is the meeting with Melchizedek, King of Salem (Jerusalem), priest of the supreme God (Genesis 14:18-20). This passage implies that Abraham has companions in faith, that his religion is not his own private invention. These companions were to be found scattered in isolated spots throughout the world, such as this small city on the way from one great center of culture on the Euphrates to another on the Nile. What is more, all along the journey, Abraham called on the name of God; he built altars and sanctuaries and taught people the nature of the divine unity. What he did amounted to a cultural revolution in his time: he tried to revive what was considered an archaic remnant of a primitive religion, and to make it into a new system of faith.

Hence, Abraham was not really an innovator or someone proclaiming an entirely new concept of religious belief. He was simply the first person in a long time to relate seriously to an old religious outlook that was primary and genuine. He was a great man in his own terms—a leader of a tribe, a successful man of the world, a conqueror in battle, a fulfilled man in private life, and a thinker who was not subdued by adverse public opinion. In other words, he was a great leader who fulfilled the same function as in later generations would be attributed to a messiah—the restoration of the ancient system of correct relations between man and the Divine.

Abraham endeavored to release the precious truth from the hands of a small body of the faithful and to build a new sort of vessel to preserve it and to live it—a tribe, a community and family structure that would become a special nation. And this national unit would be able to renew the old faith in one God and keep it alive by grouping together and living according to its spirit.

For this purpose, Abraham wandered the face of the earth, gathering to him all those people who still believed and trying to awaken others to believe in the Divine Unity. He called on the name of God and preached to all to come to God. In short, Abraham was actually the first prophet to emerge from the ancient faith who taught it as something vital and true, as something to live by.

nate to her husband. Even the great women of the Bible, women who did great deeds, were subservient to their menfolk in terms of their role and status in society. Sarah, however, enjoyed a special position—apparently as a function not only of her independent personality but also of legal-formal recognition. Her special position may derive from the fact that Abraham and Sarah were close relatives as well as husband and wife, because according to the sages, Sarah was the daughter of Haran, Abraham's elder brother. Indeed, it is explicitly written in the Bible (Genesis 20:12) that Abraham told Abimelech, King of Gerar, that Sarah was his sister, the daughter of his father, although not the daughter of his mother. Although motivated by fear, this claim is likely to have been basically true. Abraham may have been using an imprecise definition of his relationship with Sarah, describing her as his sister, because they were so very close, both in terms of kinship, as well as in other ways. Moreover *sister* was a common term of endearment for a woman in early Eastern cultures: for instance, in the Song of Songs, we find "My sister, my spouse" (5:1) and "My sister, my love" (5:2). The appellation "my sister" not only was an indication of affection but also referred to a woman of a certain status; and sister marriage was common, at least among royalty in many near-Eastern cultures, such as those of the Hittites and the Egyptians. The sister-wife was the chief wife, as opposed to the other, secondary wives who were "outsiders." In the biblical context, Sarah enjoyed the status of "sister" apparently with legal implications.

An important indication of Sarah's status and position as well as of her own forceful character is the fact that, although she was Abraham's wife and worked alongside him, she acted independently of him when circumstances required. We do not have here a man, the focal personality, around whom the action revolved, and the acquiescent or passive woman caught up in his orbit. More than this, it is obvious that, on several occasions, Abraham not only respected Sarah as his wife but also felt the need to turn to her for counsel and guidance or admitted an obligation to obtain her agreement before making a decision. We also see that from time to time Abraham acted not on his own initiative but upon instructions from Sarah. Indeed, he received a singular and unequivocal command from God: "In all that Sarah sayeth unto thee, hearken unto her voice" (Genesis 21:12). Abraham generally heeded Sarah's advice without Divine intervention, the explicit command being necessary only on the occasion of the cruel banishment of Hagar and Ishmael, Abraham's wife and child, to the wilderness.

The sages have made the interesting observation that the patriarchs were to some extent dependent on the superior prophetic powers of the matriarchs. In many biblical texts, it is clear that the women determined their family's fate, at least in relation to children and the family succession. Here the patriarchs were subordinate: it was not they who made the decisions, and it was not they who determined the shape of the great future. In every one of these cases, whether the decisions were made openly, as with Sarah, or deviously, as with Rebekah, the matriarchs acted not only as "help meet" (Genesis 2:18) but as independent personalities. At such times, it was the matriarchs who dominated, and it was their vision, their foresight, that determined family continuity and the continuity of control over the family. Sarah is even more outstanding in this respect because of her singular stature, her ability to make decisions and see them implemented.

The passage in the Bible where Abram was called by his new name, Abraham (Genesis 17:5), is both revealing and significant: Sarai, too, underwent a parallel name change and became Sarah (17:15). While we find in the Bible other name changes— as when Jacob became Israel; or Hosea ben Nun, Joshua—only one woman was granted this privilege —and that woman was Sarah. This change of name hints at a change in the whole essence of Abraham and Sarah's being, in their whole way of life. It is a profound transformation that involved them both equally, which had a double dimension, Abraham and Sarah together. One striking indica-

Sarah when she offered Abraham her servant Hagar to bear his children. This act must be understood in the cultural context of the period and by the fact that Sarah nourished a grain of hope that she, too, might benefit from this union: "It may be that I may obtain children by her" (Genesis 16:2). At the same time, Sarah's behavior reveals a deep sense of security and personal connection with her husband. She was willing for Abraham to have children by another woman because she felt certain that the ties between Abraham and herself were not dependent merely on their having children. It is interesting to compare Sarah's reaction to her barrenness with that of another biblical figure, Hannah, the mother of the prophet Samuel. Hannah could not reconcile herself to her childlessness, although her husband, Elkanah, assured her that he loved her more than ten sons. Hannah wanted, at all costs, to have a child of her own. Sarah, on the other hand, although she desired a child just as much and was happy to bear one around whom she later built her life, is shown as able to cope with the fact that she might never become a mother. She could contemplate, with at least a degree of equanimity, a situation in which Abraham's children, by her own maidservant, would be hers only by adoption. The Abraham-Sarah bond was thus personal-spiritual, not only legal-biological. They saw themselves not so much as childbearers and raisers but as a team bent on

the realization of a specific ideal. The nature of
the Abraham-Sarah relationship is evident in the
account of Hagar's first expulsion, to which Sarah
obtained Abraham's agreement, and which she
justified by saying, "I was despised in her eyes"
(16:5). Hagar despised Sarah and felt that she
could replace her; while Sarah was jealous not
because of the child, but because it seemed to her
that the servant might be usurping her place in
Abraham's affections. She would allow Hagar to
be an instrument of procreation, but would not
allow her the honor and privilege of being Abraham's beloved wife-companion.

This understanding of the idealistic aspect of
the Abraham-Sarah relationship can help to clarify
the strange episodes where Abraham appeared to
relinquish Sarah, once to Pharaoh and once to
Abimelech. Many have been troubled by Abraham's behavior, but Sarah's submission appears
even more puzzling. Clearly, her acquiescence to
Abraham's suggestion was not an expression of
passivity or surrender. Her behavior can be explained as the implementation of a joint decision.
They had decided, despite the shame and humiliation involved, that it was preferable to preserve
the wholeness of Abraham's camp—representing,
as it did, the new ideal—even at the cost of Sarah's
honor. They felt it was better to pay this awful
price, jeopardizing her own happiness and well-
being, with all that was here implied, because she

and Abraham were working together toward a specific common goal. This willingness to sacrifice her personal well-being for the common cause is surely borne out by the fact that Sarah never reproached Abraham for the injury done to her; nor, indeed, did she even mention it. In fact, when Sarah did complain to Abraham and spoke harshly to him—"My wrong be upon thee; . . . the Lord judge between me and thee" (Genesis 16:5)—it is in the quite different context of her fear that Hagar and Ishmael would take her place at Abraham's side. Sarah was willing to give up her love for, and her life with, Abraham, to be separated from him forever—but only when that separation was merely physical. What she was not willing, or able, to countenance, was spiritual separation. This is where the special essence of the Abraham–Sarah relationship is revealed, and this is why the nation of Israel has two parents: Abraham and Sarah together. It is no accident that this relationship echoes that between Adam and Eve. Abraham and Sarah are the historical-ideological-spiritual fathers of the nation, just as Adam and Eve are its biological progenitors, the two fundamental elements of the human species. This is why Abraham and Sarah saw themselves (and are thus seen by future generations) not as a couple raising a family, but as people building a society, realizing an ideal: parents of a nation. To this day, converts to the Jewish faith are called "sons of Abraham," and the women among them "daughters of Sarah," because conceptually—and, indeed, halachically—Abraham and Sarah are ideological ancestors of the Jewish nation, and all who join that nation are their children. Abraham and Sarah appear at a certain point to have all but relinquished any biological conception. Lacking physical progeny, they would beget a nation comprised of individuals united only by their new path of Divine worship.

Thus, there is added significance to the unusual biblical prophecies and reassurances that "Sarah thy wife shall bear thee a son and thou shalt call him Isaac, and I shall fulfill My covenant with him" (Genesis 17:19). The Divine message is that Abraham and Sarah must refocus on the family in order to accomplish their historic ideal.

The account of the angels' visit to Abraham announcing the coming birth of Isaac is interesting for the variety of means that the messengers used in trying to draw Sarah herself into the conversation. According to the sages, it was not the angels who spoke to Sarah, but God Himself; indeed, the Lord never spoke directly to any woman but Sarah. It seems as if this special mission, the talk with Sarah, the statement, "Nay, but thou didst laugh" (Genesis 18:15), had a deep significance because what she heard altered the whole course of her life. She had already become reconciled, and was content, with having renounced the biological aspect of womanhood. Now, she had, as it were, to be born again, with a new name, a new personality. After many years in which she had ceased to function as a woman, she was almost forcibly dragged back into the female round of pregnancy and giving birth. To a certain extent, Sarah's experiences are paralleled by the events in Abraham's life, since he was circumcised in the same year, undergoing a process of renewal, a rite of passage into a new life phase such as occurs in most societies during adolescence. Sarah, having received the angel's message of conception, underwent a renewal, a rejuvenation; and it has been said that Abraham and Sarah once again looked like young people.

Abram and Sarai had lived together for many years, during which time they worked as a team, as partners, as equals, as leaders realizing an ideal to which they were committed. When the turning point came, a new relationship was formed between them. They underwent a name change, becoming Abraham and Sarah, as an indication of rebirth. Abraham was circumcised; Sarah entered the female cycle once again. This transformation provides the symbolic meaning of the story of the patriarchs. In earlier generations, to the extent that it existed at all, spiritual influence passed from teacher to pupil. Here, this spiritual tie received a new dimension and was reinforced by the biological tie, by the birth of the child who would transmit the ideal throughout the generations of his descendants. For this reason, Abraham and Sarah were not only the spiritual forebears of the Jewish people. The meaning of the name "Children of Israel" could be made tangible only when the relationship between them underwent another level of change and became a blood tie, a biological link. It thus became the relationship that bore Isaac, in order that he, and only he, could continue the line arising from the union of Abraham and Sarah to form the nation of Israel, the Jewish people.

This biological-spiritual relationship has withstood the test of time, throughout the generations that followed. The converts of Abraham and Sarah have disappeared into history, and what has remained is the product of the strength and validity of that double bond: the Jewish nation. The dual parenthood of Abraham and Sarah remained, but only when Sarah gave birth to a child from her own womb —"Sarah thy wife shall bear thee a son indeed" (Genesis 17:19)—could they become the eternal parents of Israel in the fullest sense.

4

Isaac

THE SECOND GENERATION

saac is one of the most enigmatic characters in the Bible. And it is not so much a matter of what is said about him as it is what is left unsaid. He remains always a shadowy figure, obscure and incomplete, inviting inquiry and a desire to know more about the man behind the story.

The story itself is not long; it comprises but a few concise fragments. And the personality of Isaac that emerges in all of them is strangely puzzling, not that he ever does anything out of the ordinary. It is rather the very nature of his actions, which are more like nonactions—a doing that consists of a renunciation of doing anything.

The whole Bible story of the second of the patriarchs may be divided into six fragments: the birth

Genesis 22:1-19, 24:63-67, and 25:19-28:9.

of Isaac; the sacrifice of Isaac; the marriage of Isaac; the digging of the wells; Isaac and Abimelech; and, finally, the blessing of the two sons, Jacob and Esau. In almost all these situations, Isaac was passive; he was acted upon by others and had little or no scope for initiative. His actions were muffled and vague, as though in response to the actions of others. Altogether his personality was like an echo—not clear or definite in itself. He gave the impression of being a nonentity, one who might be called the son of his father or the father of his son.

Primarily, then, Isaac was the son of Abraham: "And these are the generations of Isaac, Abraham's son: Abraham begat Isaac" (Genesis 25:19). And almost immediately thereafter we are told that when he was at the age of threescore years, Isaac's twin sons were born, Jacob and Esau. And it would seem that the whole of this man's history is thus curtly summarized: he was the one who created Jacob who became Israel, father of the twelve tribes. Most of the deeds connected with Isaac's name were actually accomplished by other people; and what little he did on his own seems no more than a repetition, with slight variations, of what his father had done. He dug the wells that his father had dug, experienced his own version of his father's encounter with Abimelech and with Pharaoh. In other words, there was only a slight variation on the same theme; Isaac's own actions do not seem to have counted.

As for the nature of Isaac's personality, it seems to have become a profoundly moving question in terms of the whole order of biblical patriarchs and prophets. What was Isaac's role? Why is he mentioned among the great founders of the faith, not only as a link in the genealogical line but as a figure of extreme significance in himself? Who, after all, was Isaac?

To begin with, it may be pertinent to try to understand his actual individuality. And clearly, he was not one to be envied—if only as the son of such a father, with all the weight of that heritage on his shoulders. Isaac would have had to be an extraordinary person indeed to be able to make a special place for himself in such circumstances. It is known that the sons of great fathers, talented and significant as they may be in their own right, have to contend with paternal glory and, from the beginning, feel themselves inadequate, burdened with lesser or greater degrees of helplessness. History is full of many overwhelming fathers who seem to fill the entire space and leave no room for their sons to assert themselves.

This apparently was Isaac's essential problem: to find his own place in a world dominated by the genius of his father. The mission he undertook was: to carry on. And the task of the "successor" has always been one of the most unrewarding of all the tasks in history. It has often been said that "all beginnings are difficult," but continuation can be even more difficult. The capacity to persist is no less important than the power to begin. In all the significant revolutions in history, it is evident that the first generation—the revolutionaries themselves or the "founding fathers"—usually have to struggle against formidable objective forces and circumstances. But the verdict of history concerning their success, whether it was a glorious victory or merely a passing episode, lies with their successors—the generation that must stabilize and consolidate the revolution. And even if the founders are not always giants, the very fact that a person, a group, or a nation blazes a new trail endows them with superhuman stature. And yet it is the succeeding generation that has to bear the brunt of the worst of it—the backlash of the displaced old, and the relentless struggle against an unfamiliar, new reality—all without the original zeal and ardor.

Hence, one does not ascribe to the second generation the same glorious qualities that capture the imagination. The sons' task is to hold steady and not to create. Or as the Bible story puts it, they have to dig again the wells that the fathers dug before them and that have become blocked up. The father digs wells and creates new facts; time, enemies, and habit gradually fill these wells with silt. It is the son's task to go back and dig the wells again, to release the living waters and let them flow as they will.

Isaac's task, therefore, even if lacking in splendor or legendary exploits, is of utmost value and significance. And the statement "These are the generations of Isaac, . . . Abraham begat Isaac" contains the deeper meaning that, although Abraham and Isaac may be worlds apart and Abraham towers over Isaac both in personality and in the magnitude of his actions, they are nonetheless together as one—Isaac not only justifying Abraham, but establishing him forever. Thus, Isaac's achievement amounts to more than a mere contribution. By virtue of Isaac, Abraham is made what he is.

From the outset, Isaac was cared for and coddled and prepared for his task—by his mother, the servants, the herdsmen, his father. He, the one without a clearly defined face, was the most sheltered and supported of all. The reason is obvious: Abraham, the prophet and seer, had also to become the father of a great nation. And the one upon whom the responsibility devolved was Isaac. He was the one who had to make the prophecy come true; he had to be what was promised. It was not given to him to create anything new; he had only to fulfill the commitment of the previous generation. This explains the particular concern about Isaac's welfare, as is illustrated by the story of the finding of a wife for him as well as by the anxiety lest he leave the Land of Israel.

Throughout history, then—in Scripture, in legend, and in the imagination of generations of men —Isaac has personified the second generation. His inner conflicts and victories were necessarily introverted and not given to be seen. Paradoxically, were the events of his life dramatic and momentous like those of his father, he would have lost this distinction of being the true successor. In order to fill his role successfully, he had to repress any urge for assertion or self-expression. He was not allowed to be anything else, either different or something new. His destiny was to be the one who carried on.

Isaac is the symbol not of the power that breaks through limitations and creates, but of the power that conserves and maintains things in their place. Isaac endeavored to preserve the old forms, in order to keep them from getting spoiled. He showed a marked inclination toward stability, did not try any new experiments or create new forms, kept himself constantly within the aspect of the awe of God, which later, in the Kabbalah, became known as the "fear of Isaac."

Whereas Abraham was primarily a wanderer, a herdsman of sheep and camels and the like, Isaac tried to remain more or less in one place. His passivity, the "fear" of Isaac, which began at the time of his being bound for the sacrifice, was the mood of his life. It was the sign of his instrumentality; he was the trial. Isaac had to remain bound forever on the altar, the one to whom things were done because that was the entire field of his creativity. He was the background for a nation, the ground for a new reality.

This passivity was expressed in every part of his being: he remained always a tent dweller; he did not go out to find himself a wife, she was brought to him; he did not go to war, the fighting was all done for him; instead of arguing with his antagonists, he withdrew and waited for them to come to him. Even when he prayed for his sons and for the future, it was his wife Rebekah who was the dominant figure. On that occasion, when he blessed his son, we are given to understand that in his heart he seemed to prefer Esau, the son who was conspicuously the very opposite of himself. Esau symbolizes the forcefulness of precipitate action; he was a hunter, a man of the open fields, and certainly not a quiet dweller in tents. This preference of the fond father could well point to certain contradictions—or at least inner conflicts—in Isaac, which may ultimately have complemented each other. The story of the blessing throws this preference into sharp relief. The man who had always been passive and conservative retained in the core of his being a profound love for the son who was all that he, the father, was not.

Perhaps Esau represented so much of what Isaac wanted to be but, in the throes of his specific task, he could not allow himself to be. The divine election of Jacob in preference to Esau occurred within a closed system of immense forces, unimaginably vast objectives, in which Isaac was only a single factor, remaining passive and letting things take their course. This incredible complexity is beyond human conception; but, though driven by higher forces, it nevertheless did include Isaac's likes and dislikes—his preference for venison and for his son the hunter—just as it included his blindness, the dual nature of his offspring, the character of his wife, the whole context of the resolute life he had led.

The conclusion to the blessing incident seems, therefore, to have a clear meaning. It was Jacob who had to succeed Isaac. However, Isaac, as an individual person, in all the private humanity of his feelings, would have liked it to be otherwise, would have liked the successor to be more like his active son and his active father, the man of open power and victory. Isaac could not see the potential of his tent-dweller son Jacob, who seemed to be no more than a copy of himself. In fact, Isaac may have had reason to be anxious that Jacob might simply carry on as he himself had done, without daring to make any innovations, knowing or intuitively aware that such a repetition of himself could not continue without endangering the future. The next generation—each has its own task—would have to be ready for the fresh conquests that follow a period of entrenchment. After him, he felt that someone like Esau should lead the way and break through into new territory.

Isaac's assumption was correct, but he misread the true personalities involved. The very initiative shown by Jacob in trying to get the blessing for himself is proof that he was not a copy of his passive father. It is the clue to the essence of Jacob: he who will fight fiercely to gain only those ends he considers important.

In such manner, a closed circle is formed—paradox within paradox. When Jacob put on the hairy garments of Esau, he was not dressing himself up as another; he was really showing his father his own dual nature. Jacob was not a copy of Isaac, nor was he a throwback to Abraham; he was a synthesis, an integration of both Abraham and Isaac. As such, Jacob was also the one who made it possible for something new to take place. He was the keeper of tradition who was also an innovator. Jacob was the hidden one; what was visible of him was only an image, a rather pale figure of what could become meaningful. It was only later, when he revealed himself as the one capable of acting and taking responsibility for the action of others, when he strove with men and angels—only then was he worthy of the blessing.

After all, Isaac wanted as his successor someone with these very qualities of boldness, initiative, astuteness, and tenacity, and he believed that Esau was the more likely to have them. Isaac was even prepared to forgo all Jacob's gentleness of spirit, his nobility of mind, for the vanquishing temper of Esau. When, however, Jacob showed that he contained within himself these fighting qualities as well—when he brought home meat—in one form or another, he justified the blessing. Thus, when Isaac later sent Jacob away to find himself a wife from among the kinsmen of Abraham, it may be gathered that Isaac was finally convinced that Jacob was strong enough to leave the sheltering borders of the Land and the family tribe and to forge his own way.

Even as Isaac learned of the deception practiced on him, and while he was still stunned with shock and surprise, he nevertheless maintained, "And he shall be blessed" (Genesis 27:33). The fact that Jacob was not merely the "good boy," the nice tent dweller, but also the stealer of the blessing somehow legitimized the blessing, so that Isaac, even in his mortification, could say, "Yes, and he shall be blessed."

5

Rebekah

THE WHITE SHEEP IN
THE FAMILY

ebekah appears in only a few scenes in the Bible, each time in a different light. Once she is a young girl drawing water; once a pregnant woman going to ascertain the future; and once again, a mother sending her son Jacob to Padan-aram. In each of these cases, the predominating factor is Rebekah's total confidence in all that she does. She displays a consistency, a certainty, and a commitment to whatever she believes to be right. This resoluteness is Rebekah's most outstanding characteristic.

The first time we meet Rebekah (Genesis 24:15-28), she is behaving in the manner that was to characterize her throughout her life: without pretention, with the same wholeheartedness that

---

Genesis 24:15-67, 25:19-26:12, and 27:1-46.

marked her later actions in maturity, although she was still very, very young here. She received the stranger from a distant land with extraordinary grace, going to the great trouble of watering all the thirsty camels until they "had done drinking" (24:22). She then introduced herself to the stranger and told him that her parents "have both straw and provender enough, and room to lodge in" (24:25). At this point she knew nothing of who her guest was or of his significance for her future life. Nonetheless, she assumed responsibility: the camels would be watered; their owner would drink and, with his servants, would have a place to spend the night in her father's house.

This ability to reach the right conclusion and to act accordingly is prominent in the interesting incident that occurred after the servant revealed the reason for his coming and the significance of his meeting with Rebekah. Her brother and father, Laban and Bethuel, had agreed in principle to her union with Isaac, but they procrastinated, tried to delay things, her mother and brother suggesting that she "abide with us a year or ten months" (Genesis 24:55). In the end, they said, "We will call the damsel, and enquire at her mouth" (24:57). We have here not an explicit refusal, merely a hint of caution and of warning. They were relying on the girl's confusion and fear of the future to make her hesitate and thus gain time. However, this damsel, young as she was, had no doubts. She decided, probably to the great surprise of her family, that she was leaving at once with the stranger, for his home in a distant land, because she knew that this was what she must do. This impression of decisiveness is confirmed in the short account of the first meeting between Rebekah and Isaac. Having traveled for days, she saw a man in a field and decided that this was *the* man. She certainly would not have asked about each and every man that she had met on her way, but this one, she sensed, was special: "What man is this that walketh in the field?" (24:65). She knew exactly what he was and what her role should be. This then is Rebekah, the epitome of decisiveness. Whether it is a moment to express benevolence or love, or to decide which son is worthy of blessing, she makes a quick, sharp, and comprehensive decision with no trace of hesitancy.

In this sense Rebekah stands in contrast to Isaac, and in many ways complements his personality. Isaac is fundamentally a person who does *not* make decisions, a person to whom things happen. In his first great test, the binding on the altar (Genesis 22:1–18), Isaac did not act but was acted upon. He did not go to seek a wife; a wife was brought to him. Later, at every stage of his life, it was Rebekah who decided and acted with complete self-confidence, whereas Isaac was hesitant and unsure. When it was necessary to ask God the meaning of the conflict in her womb, she did not send her husband but went herself to seek guidance (25:22-23). What is more, she kept to herself the information she received and from it drew her own conclusions.

At the same time, it is interesting that, with all her resolution of will, Rebekah made no attempt to dominate her partner, to trample on his personality. She did not try to take on herself things that were outside her own province. She not only loved her husband; she revered him. When Rebekah sent Jacob to receive Isaac's blessing, one senses—for all the deviousness involved—the foundation of trust and admiration. It was very clear to Rebekah that Isaac was righteous and saintly, and that his blessing would hold good, and thus she did her utmost to ensure that the right son was blessed. We have here both admiration for Isaac and a knowledge of his limitations. She might attempt to lead him, but not in all things, and never beyond her own point of certainty.

Rebekah was a woman of great understanding. When she felt an inner clarity, she was capable of moving anyone who stood in her way: family, parents, relatives. Yet there is nothing domineering or destructive in this decisiveness. Time and again she did what she felt she had to do and then retired to her place backstage.

The sages viewed the matriarchs as having prophetic powers, superior to those of the patriarchs; and Rebekah did indeed act as prophet, in response to a revelation that pierced the veil of the present. Hers was a condition not of constant prescience but of flashes of exalted clarity, consistent with Maimonides' description of prophecy as a stroke of lightning revealing the route to be taken. In this sense, at all the crucial moments of her life, Rebekah had a clarity of vision greater than that of those around her.

She knew that she must water the camels; she knew that she must go with the stranger, Abraham's servant, that this was her fate. When she saw Isaac, she knew that this was *the* man; and when she bore his sons, she knew which of them should receive the birthright. At each moment of intervention, Rebekah was sharply cognizant not only of the immediate situation but also of the future, although, as the sages point out, she did not always fully understand her own prophetic message.

An important clue to Rebekah's character is given in the passage where she was introduced as "Rebekah, the daughter of Bethuel the Syrian at Padan-aram, the sister to Laban the Syrian" (Genesis 25:20). This triple emphasis on her origins—whose daughter she was and whose sister, as well as where she came from—is very significant. Rebekah was one of those not infrequent cases of a gifted child growing up in a family that, despite aristocratic ancestry, is itself in decline. We see a hint of this degeneracy in the feeble character of

Bethuel, the father, who seems to have abdicated his role in favor of his son, Laban, the decisive figure in the family. We learn more about Laban, in later chapters of Genesis, concerning his relationship with Jacob, Rebekah's son. Reading between the lines of the biblical narrative, we can ascertain that the family had its unsavory side. At the time of Rebekah's marriage to Isaac, it probably still retained something of its outward pretensions even while declining into a life of poverty, of petty cheating, of dishonor.

Of the two branches of the family of Terah, Abraham's line (and those family members who joined him) grew increasingly great and powerful, while the other side, that of Nahor, was deteriorating, depleting its resources, preoccupied with pettiness as it sank into decay. Rebekah, therefore, is an atavistic figure, portrayed as containing within herself the strength and vitality of the great line from which the patriarchs were descended. In the mixture of different strains, she was the healthy person in a sick family. And the healthy, bright child in a degenerate, flawed family is a gift from heaven. In Rebekah's case, it is she who had to be the one to make quick, sharp decisions, because no one in her environment was trustworthy. She had to be the one to determine the course of events, while her menfolk were absorbed in "wheeling and dealing." From childhood, she had learned that the responsibility rested with her, and this characteristic resolution remained with her throughout her life.

In this sense, too, Rebekah was the opposite of Isaac, who grew up surrounded by trustworthy folk: "Isaac, Abraham's son: Abraham begat Isaac" (Genesis 25:19). He had an aristocratic mother and a father of the noblest character, an old retainer of incorrigible integrity, and other faithful servants. Isaac's world was supportive, secure; he could hesitate or even err because there were always others, loving and concerned, to back him up. This supportive environment had another aspect: Isaac knew little of the world of evil and deceit, because his immediate world was harmonious and whole. Rebekah, on the other hand, grew up in a world whose failings she knew all too well. "Rebekah, the daughter of Bethuel, sister to Laban" is understood by the sages as "the daughter of a scoundrel and the sister of a scoundrel." She had learned the meaning of cheating, of hypocrisy; and this knowledge lay at the root of the difference between Rebekah and Isaac and their relationship to their sons.

Isaac was an "easy victim" of duplicity; he was neither suspicious nor afraid because there was no dishonesty in his own heart. He therefore took his children at face value. The well-behaved, active son was for him also good and dutiful; Isaac did not see beyond the façade. Rebekah, however, was an expert in such matters. She knew that people could be duplicitous, and the resemblance that is common between a man and his maternal uncle she distinguished in Esau and Laban. She recognized her own family in Esau, and she knew his shortcomings and his weak points. It is not said in the Scriptures that Rebekah did not love Esau, and certainly not that she hated him; simply, she was far more discerning than Isaac. Isaac was overwhelmingly the innocent victim (pure offering) who is outside the context of this world, while Rebekah was very much part of it. She was perhaps the archetype of generations of Jewish mothers who had to struggle for their existence, and even more, for the survival of their children in a harsh and ruthless world.

Since Rebekah was born into a family that was close to the margins of society, she had to develop her strong personality, her ability to act confidently and decisively, because if she were not resolute, there was no one who would act in her stead. She knew the world, knew its limitations and its hardships, yet the fact that she recognized evil did not corrupt her; rather, she herself cultivated an admiration for what is good, pure, and innocent. Thus, the relationship between Rebekah and Isaac acquired additional significance: for her, he represented another world, a higher level of being than she had known; she was bound to him and perhaps loved him because of his purity. She might have been required to deceive him now and then, but always for his own good, to spare him error and injury. It was characteristic of Rebekah that she did not tell Isaac that he was wrong in his assessment of his sons, and that she believed Esau to be unreliable. She manipulated Isaac into blessing Jacob instead of Esau out of her love for Isaac, in an attempt to shield and protect him from the emotional shock of his own error.

Isaac knew evil only from afar; Rebekah, from close up. Her life was a personal victory over her environment, her origins, her birth, and she tried thereafter throughout her life to adhere to what was essentially good: the good family, the continuity of the good line. And if others, including her husband, were not able to ensure this condition, she, who knew the pain and ugliness of evil, would have to be the one to perpetuate her own personal victory: the victory of light that emanates from the darkness.

6

Rachel

THE UNFULFILLED DREAM

achel is, in many ways, the mother figure of the Jewish people. From what is told about her in the Book of Genesis, and even more, in later Scripture and literature, she has come to represent the feminine side of the Jewish people in one aspect of its being. Despite the fact that the large majority of the Jewish people are not descendants of Rachel, she remains their symbol of national existence.

Rachel's place in the national consciousness is not so much a function of the story of her life in Genesis, but rather of the haunting imagery of Jeremiah, "Rachel weeping for her children refused to be comforted" (Jeremiah 31:15). Jeremiah's Rachel is the mother who cradles the nation, the one to whom the child pours out his heart. Not

Genesis 29:4-30, 30:1-25, 31:1-55, and 35:16-20.

for naught did Rachel's Tomb become a magnet for so many generations of wretched and forlorn Jews who have felt the need to weep before God, sensing somehow that Mother Rachel will understand their tears, sorrow, and pain.

One aspect of this tender understanding of pain is that she herself was yearning for an unfulfilled dream. The story of Rachel the woman and her relationship with Jacob have something of this quality of yearnings that are never fully realized. Rachel represents expectation; she represents dreams and aspirations. However, she remains forever expectant, forever awaiting fulfillment. Both personally and symbolically, she is perhaps one of the most poignant expressions of the person who has everything—and yet remains lacking. Even when Rachel's dreams were realized, it was not in her lifetime: the hope, the potential remained always suspended between what might have been and what might yet come to be.

From the time when, as we are told, "and Jacob loved Rachel" (Genesis 29:18) until her death with the birth of Benjamin, just as the family came to settle in the Land, Rachel's life held much pain and frustration. The uneven satisfactions of a timeless love could not mitigate the sadness caused by the near realization of aspirations and hopes that seemed always to be snatched from her grasp just at the moment of fulfillment. One powerful example of this frustration lay in the fact that, although Rachel was Jacob's first love, she was not "the wife of his youth." The sages have commented on the special bond between a man and the first woman he knows. This bond existed not between Jacob and Rachel, but between Jacob and Leah. Indeed, the whole Jacob-Rachel relationship, despite their great love, was subject to the constant strains of unfulfilled expectation. Even more than in an ordinary marriage, the consummation of love in motherhood was meaningful here: it was supremely important to give birth to a bearer of blessings, an heir to a glorious tradition. But Rachel remained with a yearning that was unfulfilled, while her sister Leah gave birth to son after son.

Rachel came very close to the fulfillment of her dreams, but their ultimate realization was always snatched from her. When Jacob finally managed to extricate himself from the clutches of Laban, and when, freed of the fear of Esau, he achieved the first moment of tranquillity in the Promised Land, it appeared as though Rachel, too, would finally achieve her dreams. She bore a son, Joseph, and anticipated, "The Lord shall add to me another son" (Genesis 30:24). But when that other son was born, instead of fulfillment and happiness, it was death that came to her. Rachel thus became the personification of the tragic aspect of the people of Israel.

As the mother of the nation, which did not, after all, issue entirely from her offspring, Rachel weeping for her sons is suited to see the tragic future of exile and suffering. It is exile that, in fact, epitomizes the grief of Rachel: whether it is for a homeland won and later snatched away; or whether it is for long years of waiting for the consummation of a youthful love; or whether it is death at the moment of fulfillment. Therefore, for many centuries during the First and Second Temple periods, and certainly after the destruction of the Temple, Rachel came to symbolize the *Shekhinah* in exile.

The above notwithstanding, Rachel, the woman, also displayed some quite different character traits. The biblical story discloses relatively more about her relationship with Jacob than about other men and women, and reveals a certain weakness of character, especially when juxtaposed with her sister, Leah. Rachel knew full well that she was loved and was so confident of her position that more than once she took excessive advantage of it. In this sense, she personified another aspect of the Jewish nation: its feeling of being chosen, its overconfidence in the love of God, which often led to disaster.

Not only did Rachel not court Jacob in the way that Leah did; but more than once, she actually came into conflict with him. The only time Jacob reprimanded one of his wives was when he impatiently rebuked Rachel in a way that also implied a subtle protest at her vaunting her mastery over him.

Throughout his life, Jacob remained steadfast under all circumstances. Even where he had good reason for anger, he restrained himself, sometimes over many years. Only in this one instance, when Rachel demanded that he give her sons, did he lose patience.

This plea for Jacob's intervention to end her barrenness indicates that Rachel recognized that Jacob was more than just a successful herdsman or man of affairs. She saw in him, just as Leah did, a figure who was beyond the ordinary, who was a man of God.

The way in which Rachel tried to take advantage of her privileged position reveals a certain weakness of character, the same weakness or surrender to temptation that is revealed in the temporary "exchange" of Jacob for the mandrakes, and in the stealing of the household gods. She was rescued from this entanglement, as she was saved from Jacob's anger and from her other difficulties, by a mixture of luck, charm, and daring. Nonetheless, the weakness existed: time and again Rachel abuses her privileges because she is so secure in the knowledge that nothing could harm her relationship with Jacob. In this sense, too, Rachel is "daughter of Jerusalem . . . daughter of Zion" (Lamentations 2:13), not only because she was the young love, the "partner" of the Lord (the accepted image throughout the Bible), but because she was also the wayward and capricious

woman. Here again, Rachel has been the archetype of the people of Israel for most of its history,
during the period of the Kingdom of Judah and
Israel and at various times later. She represents
the feeling that—do what we will—in the end, we
are the favored ones. No matter how shameful our
deeds, the love of God will be forthcoming to us
and not to others.

The relationship between Jacob and Rachel thus
became a paradigm of the great, loving, historical
relationship between God and Israel. The sages
relate to those moments when Rachel unthink-
ingly renounced Jacob because of her certainty
that he was hers. They point out that Jacob's un-
witting curse that the stealer of the idols would
die was fulfilled in Rachel, who died in childbirth
shortly thereafter. That is, love with all its exaltation, with all its obstacle-shattering force, nevertheless does have its restrictions. Some transgress-
ing cannot be justified, even by the chosen one
with all the charm, the beauty, and the allure of
love. In other words, the love for Israel is real, and
the Divine bond constant, eternal, and unbreakable, yet sin nevertheless begets punishment at
every level.

It may be appropriate to compare Jacob's rela-
tionship with Rachel with the similar story of
Elkanah, the father of Samuel, and his two wives,
Hannah and Peninah. Peninah had children, and
Hannah did not; but Elkanah's preference for Han-

nah was clear and unquestioning. He told Hannah that he was better for her than ten sons. Jacob, on the other hand, never went so far; he never indicated that he was willing to risk Leah, or to cancel his commitment and his obligations to her, or to say explicitly and brutally that he preferred either sister. The reason was not that he did not love Rachel. His love for her is clear throughout their story, not only in Rachel's lifetime but also after her death; and his special relationship to her became a significant factor in the family saga as expressed by Jacob's attachment to Joseph and to Benjamin as well as by the blessings Jacob bestowed on the sons of Joseph. The source of the difference lies in the fact that Rachel did not recognize limitations; she lived in a sphere where love justified everything. Unlike Hannah, whose sorrow and longing were turned inward on herself, Rachel beguiled herself with the assurance that her bond with Jacob would never be severed, and that she could therefore do as she liked. It was this attitude that riled Jacob's anger and that affected his overall relationship with his wives.

Ultimately, Leah is placed on par with Rachel, and at times even at an advantage. Although Rachel was the one that Jacob desired—perhaps the only one that he truly desired—she forfeited the exclusivity of their relationship. For a love that is liberated from restraint, that sees only its rights and not its duties, brings about a crisis. In this sense, Rachel symbolizes a reality that is true of all human relationships, whether among individuals, families, or nations. Even a great love requires limitations, a yoke of discipline and commitment.

Deviation from that commitment ends in punishment. No breach of this discipline can vanish without trace, evoking no response. Thus, the later image of Rachel, that of the mother weeping for her children, is the lasting one and completes the other image of Rachel, the young wife. She personifies the sorrow of the limitations of being chosen, of the barriers to total love. Rachel, the mythical personification of the nation of Israel mourning for her children as she anticipates their return from exile, is a recapitulation as well as a rectification of the life of Rachel the woman.

Still, for the people of Israel as well as for Rachel the woman, there is return and comfort. Jacob's anger, as well as his curse, does not terminate the relationship. There is punishment, but it does not result in eternal abandonment and oblivion. "There is hope in thine end" and in the promise that "thy children shall come again to their own border" (Jeremiah 31:17).

7

Leah

THE SPOUSE AND MOTHER

eah was, in many ways, the most unfortunate of the matriarchs. We meet her first in the Bible as the sister of Rachel, with her aura of beauty, charm, and romantic love. Leah then becomes Jacob's wife through error, perpetually a woman of subordinate status. Nor is she as attractive as her younger sister. All of these render Leah a secondary character in the biblical account, a substitution. Leah's tragedy is that her husband also perceives her in this light: a woman whom he never considered became a replacement for his true beloved. She can never establish her own truly intimate relationship with her husband.

Another source of Leah's pain and sorrow stems from the fact that she herself does not view her marriage to Jacob as an accident, a marriage of

Genesis 29:16–30, 30:1-20.

convenience, or a mere concession to family or societal norms. From numerous biblical incidents and exchanges, it is apparent that Leah—perhaps more than Rachel—is committed to Jacob, wants him, and loves him. But her love goes unrequited. Leah is for Jacob an outcome of fraud and deception, the wife of a mistaken marriage. It is only after many years, if at all, that Jacob fully relates to her. Leah, then, is the archetype of a woman in love who is never loved in return with the same depth and passion.

However, the sages have already pointed out that Jacob's attitude to Leah was by no means unequivocally one of scorn, loathing, or hatred. The laconic statement "And he loved also Rachel more than Leah" (Genesis 29:30) is our only clear indication of the nature of their relationship. We do not have here a woman who was abhorred in contrast to one who was loved. Jacob's feelings for Leah were not at all clear-cut: he preferred Rachel but was by no means indifferent to her older sister. Simply, despite her perennial desire for greater intimacy, for greater love, he always maintained a degree of reserve and distance; and at the human level, Leah's sorrow was never fully resolved.

There is, however, another aspect to the story. In the Bible, the events are seen subjectively, through the eyes of the people involved, and objectively, in the context of their historical implications.

In this context, the Leah-Rachel relationship has had an enduring influence on the structure of Jewish nationhood, first revealed in the antagonism between the sons of Leah and Rachel's son, Joseph. Later, it became one of the factors in the great historical rivalry between Leah's tribes, led by Judah, and Rachel's tribes, led by Joseph's son Ephraim. It was repeated in all the conflicts and clashes between the kingdom of Judah and the kingdom of Israel-Samaria, and it was only with the almost total disappearance of the tribe of Ephraim that a certain unity was created. To this day, the Jewish nation—remnant of the kingdom of Judah—reflects this duality: it consists of Judah, the son of Leah, and Benjamin, the son at whose birth Rachel died. Ezekiel's prophecy of redemption as the union of the tree of Ephraim and the tree of Judah is an idea that recurs in many prophetic visions. Historically, it has not been realized in the context of all the sons of both Leah and Rachel. In a sense, therefore, this ancient rivalry will continue until the End of Days, when, as it is prophesied, there will be two messiah-redeemers: Messiah Son of Joseph and Messiah Son of David.

Through the ages, it has become more and more apparent that the house of Israel is descended from the sons of Leah, while Rachel's line has become a branch, an embellishment of the national heritage, yet less significant in substance and function. Leah's house has provided, on the one hand, national continuity through the house of David, the descendants of Judah, and, on the other, the continuity of religion through the priesthood and, to some extent also, the prophecy, through Leah's son Levi. In historical perspective, it is Leah who became the Mistress of the House, the mainstay of the family from whom the nation stems.

Leah's ultimate position as Jacob's wife is reflected also in the fact that of the four wives—Leah, Rachel, Bilhah, Zilpah—only one was buried beside Jacob in the cave of Machpelah, and that one was Leah. In other words, at the end of her life, Jacob, too, recognized Leah's role: he realized that ultimately the people of Israel would be descended from her sons and not from Rachel's.

The Leah-Rachel relationship has been a subject for study far in excess of the personal story of the two sisters. It has become the basis for a comparison of two worldviews. In philosophy and Kabbalah, Rachel and Leah symbolize respectively the *Shekhinah* in exile and the *Shekhinah* redeemed. The "Higher Lady" is Leah; the "Lower Lady" is Rachel. Contrary perhaps to the popular image in Genesis, Rachel appears as the weeping woman, while Leah is the "happy mother of sons," positions reflected in the respective liturgies of "Tikkun Rachel" and "Tikkun Leah." In the broadest sense, the relationship between Jacob and Leah is not only the more enduring but in a certain way also the more correct and the more complete.

This is a case where a mistaken act proves to have been the right one, and the dream—simply a dream. The great love with all its passion, its romanticism and attraction, was not in fact the "right" love. The pragmatic, down-to-earth bond between Leah and Jacob, manifested through the bearing and rearing of sons who comprised the bulk of the House of Jacob, proved to be the more basic, authentic, and permanent connection between Jacob and his wife. Ultimately, it is Leah who is the consummate wife. We have here a not-so-unusual situation where emotions—particularly of an emotionally involved man—pull in one direction, while more clearheaded and incisive reasoning would lead in a very different direction.

The relationship between Jacob and his two chief wives, Rachel and Leah, is by no means simple. Fundamentally, we have here two kinds of love in all their complexity: The first is a romantic love that draws its sustenance from longing, from separation and distance, from premature death—a love full of expectations, dreams, and memories. On the other hand, we have the love of a faithful woman, the woman who remains beside her husband, works, and struggles in the daily round with him, bears him most of his children, and whose love is constant, stable, and real. Leah's relationship with Jacob was without the drama, the elation, and the dejection that characterized his love for Rachel. In a sense, she was the romantic plaything; Leah, the mature and faithful wife.

This essential difference between Leah and Rachel is somehow expressed in the curious incident of the mandrakes (Genesis 30:14–16). Leah's son Reuben found mandrakes in a field, and Rachel expressed her desire for them. The sages have indicated that although mandrakes were considered an aphrodisiac, this belief was connected only with the root of the plant, and never with its fruit, which was regarded as a plaything, an amusement, because of its pleasant smell and appearance. That is to say, Rachel desired a bauble of some kind; and although mandrakes were fairly common, she was willing to renounce Jacob for one night in exchange for this trifle. Leah, on the other hand, declared bitterly that Rachel sought to take from her "my husband and wouldst thou take away my son's mandrakes also?" Leah was, however, more than willing to trade the plant for the man. She was even prepared to suffer the humiliating statement to Jacob that "surely I have earned thee with my son's mandrakes," a statement purposely ambiguous. Leah here revealed her deeper tie to Jacob, one that went beyond human passion. This was a deep love, a profound and intimate relationship, which expressed a longing for close communion with her husband. Each of the names she gave her newborn sons was both a plea for Jacob's love and a declaration that the newborn confirmed her bond with him. The sages have commented on the story of the mandrakes that because Rachel belittled her husband's bed in this way, she was not buried beside him. For them the anecdote of the mandrakes symbolized the entire relationship between Jacob and his wives.

Lacking the charm, the amusement, and the spontaneous affection of Rachel, Leah in the biblical story is the image of the sorrowing woman involved in a desperate struggle to win Jacob's love, to grow closer to him. Her sons were one of the means to this end. The Jacob–Leah relationship is therefore seen as being deeper, more stable, and more productive than it appears on the surface, both in itself and in the historical context. Each one of Leah's sons expresses a different aspect of Jacob's personality, a different aspect of his character. They come together in the wider context of the Jewish people throughout history. During the course of that history, the relations between the tribes of Leah and Rachel reflect the relations between the sisters themselves: Rachel's descendants, like Joshua, Saul, and even Mordecai, were themselves great leaders, but they did not create permanent dynasties. Theirs are chance associations, impressive but ephemeral. The lasting connection perpetuated from generation to generation is that passing from Leah, through the house of David. It is the essence of the personal relationship between Leah and Jacob.

The beauty, the charm, the passionate involvement are Rachel's. The intimate bond, the love that is accompanied by fidelity, by continuity—and, therefore, by a measure of the eternal—is Leah's.

8

Joseph

THE MASTER OF DREAMS

n Jewish literature, Joseph is known as the *Tzadik*, or wholly exemplary man, the prototype of a righteous saint. At the feast of Tabernacles, among the seven patriarchs and prophets who each come to the *sukkah* as invited guest, Joseph the *Tzadik* figures prominently. In the Bible, however, Joseph is a strange and unpredictable figure, in spite of all the assurance and comfort evoked by the story itself.

The basis for considering Joseph the archetypal *tzadik* is drawn from the climax of the story of the wife of Potiphar, whose temptations he firmly resisted. Especially when one compares it with similar incidents involving his older brothers—Reuben (with Bilhah) and Judah (with Tamar)—Joseph's self-control stands out. What is more, he was

---

Genesis 37:1-36, 39:1-48:22, and 50:1-26.

young and alone and more severely tried than they, besides being fully aware of the penalty he would have to pay for his virtue. His behavior was, therefore, truly exemplary; and, in this respect, he may be said to be deserving of the title *tzadik*.

But, of course, the title has far wider implications; and in later literature and in the Kabbalah, Joseph is recognized as a *tzadik* in terms of one whose self-control becomes a source of power and influence over all that is in his domain, from the physical and personal to the spiritual and the social. The *tzadik* is someone who knows when to give and when not to give: the one who can be the generous provider of the people, and the one who can also withstand the temptation either to bestow good or to refrain from giving. The capacity to control one's natural propensities is one of the main characteristics of the *tzadik* and makes it possible for him to be that strangely double personality, saint and ruler. And every *tzadik* is in a way both saint and sovereign, not only able to resist temptation but also capable of boundless giving as an act of grace as well as of control over all manner of situations.

Insofar as the exemplary qualities of Joseph blend into the folklore tradition of the *tzadik* as a type, all is well. But what about the questionable sides of the Joseph we learn about in the Bible? Those aspects that induced violent reactions from his brothers, for instance? The brothers not only failed to understand Joseph, but he exasperated them; there was something about Joseph that aroused a fiercely negative response as well as a positive one. And it was not only what he said or did; it was the very nature of his personality. The fact that his father, Jacob, spoke aloud in open praise of his favorite son would not in itself have aroused such venomous jealousy if it had not added fuel to an already existing dislike. Joseph himself was the problem; he was a stumbling block and a constant focus for complaint by the very fact of his being what he was.

However that may have been, Joseph did not for long remain a shepherd boy. Soon enough, whether as *tzadik* or as the leader of a tribe, he began to turn into a legendary patriarch. Evidently, the trials and tribulations in Egypt effected some sort of crisis and change. His better qualities came to the fore, while the more disagreeable ones dissolved into the past. Nevertheless, even in his greatness, there remained something strange and inexplicable. Even after Joseph appeared to have outgrown the problems of his childhood and youth and had become a successful leader of men, his response on meeting his brothers is reminiscent of that old incalculable, exasperating aspect. The oddly dramatic staging of the meeting, contrived and premeditated, almost as if it were a modern comedy, is a story that ends happily enough. But it is not always so funny. There is a distinct note of grief and long-repressed anger. To be sure, the comic features may be considered as secondary to a larger, tragic drama. And thus we may have a clue to that strange quality of Joseph. For even his relations with others—with Potiphar, with the wife of Potiphar, with Pharaoh, and so on—tend to be extreme and out of the ordinary. How did he manage to inspire such complete faith and affection? Whence his power over people, and what did he do with it? In what direction did he continually turn?

The key to Joseph's personality may lie in that first of the labels given him—"dreamer." This epithet confers on Joseph the character of an agent, of one who transmits, even if with his own complexity. He was not a prophet and thus differed from Jacob. His father Jacob was a prophet figure who saw God in his dream, with angels, ladder to the sky, the opening of the heavens, the future of the nation, whereas, although Joseph was unlike his earthy brothers, who had no visions at all, he was also not a prophet like his father. Joseph simply had a certain propensity for seeing things in dreams.

The prophet Jeremiah tried to emphasize this propensity when—in contrast to the passage in Deuteronomy, "If there arise among you a prophet or a dreamer of dreams" (13:1)—he said, "The prophet that hath a dream, let him tell a dream; and he that hath My word, let him speak My word

faithfully. What is chaff to the wheat?" (Jeremiah
23:28). In other words, there is an intermediate
stage, in which a person is not a prophet and yet
has visions, dreams meaningful dreams. And this
is indeed the special quality of Joseph's, that
strange and inexplicable quality that had much
significance for his own phenomenal growth as
well as for other figures in the whole of human
history.

The significance of the dream as an expression
of wish is an ancient discovery; and Freud did no
more than probe scientifically into what has long
been common knowledge of a certain kind, as
repeatedly mentioned in the Bible and the Talmud. At the same time, although it was known
by the ancients that the dream was largely a subjective phenomenon, they also were aware of the
existence of another kind of dream—the prophetic
dream. They believed that certain dreams can be
a means for revealing the unknown, whether in
the individual soul or in the highest mystery of
existence. The difficulty is that the experiences
of the prophet and the dreamer are not clearly
distinguishable; it is very much a matter of the
level of clarity and personal involvement. If the
prophet is a genuine seer, his clarity of vision is
absolutely objective and separate from his individual personality. He can be either more or less
conscious of the source of his prophetic message;
he is not at all identified with it. A prophet may

even be wretched about his prophecy, be surprised by it and unhappy about it, even struggle against it. He cannot suppress it.

The dreamer is in a much more delicate and intricate situation. He never reaches the level of prophetic clarity, even though he may be in close touch with genuine aspects of the soul, not only with those forming the background for hidden or manifest desires but also with those that could be the source of higher powers and visions. As the sages put it, in their characteristic idiom, there is a difference between dream prophecy from an angel and dream prophecy from a demon, depending on whether the dream springs from the higher or the lower impulses in a person.

In this sense, the problem of the dreamer is the unfinished nature of his vision. He may be far beyond the wishful thinking of fantasy without yet approaching the objective clarity of prophecy. Hence, the great dreamers have often been in profound conflict about the authenticity of their visions. Even Jacob, after his momentous dream of the ladder to heaven, made the astonishing statement: "If God will be with me, and will keep me in this way that I go . . . then shall the Lord be my God" (Genesis 28:20-21). Making the conditions would be odd if Jacob really believed the prophetic truth of the dream and did not wonder whether it might not be a matter of wishful thinking. He left the final judgment to later years, when it would have indeed become obvious to him that it was a prophetic dream; twenty years and more had to elapse before he returned to the same spot and set up an altar at Beth-el.

Joseph, however, seems not to have had much doubt about the prophetic quality of his dreams. When he saw the sheaves bowing before him, he was convinced that they foretold something of the future. He, therefore, told it to his brothers, desiring, in all innocence, to have them participate in this valid insight. Indeed, we can imagine what might have taken place had the brothers accepted the truth of the vision and made themselves receptive to the inevitable overlordship of Joseph. The whole story might have proceeded along another, far less tragic course. The problem, however, is that the dreamer himself is rarely completely convinced of the authenticity of his dream, even when, at best, he does not allow doubts to enter. In the case of Joseph, the brothers were certainly unable to see his dream as anything other than a subjective expression of a personal wish for power.

Whence the ambivalence in dreams? Who, after all, is the dreamer? Was Joseph just a bemused young man with fantasies of greatness who dreamed his reveries of the day? Or was he the object of extraordinary visions that came to him, either wittingly or unwittingly, and transported him into an unknown future?

Indeed, Joseph's dreams remained unresolved

for many years. When he was first sold as a slave, he was probably desolate in the certainty that his dream had been no more than a wish fulfillment. Only when he reached greatness was he able to observe that his dreams may have been true visions. Then was the appropriate time to reveal himself to his brothers. But Joseph did not do so at once: he waited for additional years to pass, doubtless under the influence of that other aspect of his personality.

Only when Joseph emerged completely from the status of slave to that of servant and then to master of the kingdom, when he was quite sure that not only the sheaves, but the very sun and the moon bowed down before him, could he be absolutely certain about the nature of that youthful dream. He then had to act out the drama of that dream to its logical conclusion. What might have been the private daydream of a youth had become a profound prophecy. The sheaves had come to him; the very sun and the moon would have to appear and bow to him. The intricate interplay of forces was no longer entirely dependent on him; the drama was not his to direct. Some other fact was involved. And Joseph at this point ceased to be "dreamer of dreams."

After the despair of the moment when he was sold as a slave, he became the slave of his dreams; he had to realize them. An examination of the relationship of Joseph to various later dreams shows that he viewed them not only as something to be manipulated or conjured up at will but as true signs of the future. He may have endeavored, for a while at least, to struggle with this insight and adapt it, to make it amenable. Unlike the unalterable and absolute nature of prophecy, the dream is flexible and can be adjusted, if only to a limited degree. Nevertheless, even the dream has to be fulfilled.

And this is true of the dreams of other people as well, especially of Pharaoh, whose dreams became the basis of all Joseph's actions for many years of his life. He endeavored to cope with the destiny of Egypt by living out Pharaoh's dream of the fat and the lean cows, the sheaves devouring one another. Joseph did not try to convert the good years into anything else or to pretend that the difficult years would soon be over. He kept to the scheme of seven consecutive years and preserved what he could—relying completely on his own experience of dealing with dreams: that is, how to live out the dream and not struggle against it, to be receptive to its inevitability and yet to come to grips with the real problems it imposes.

In his boyhood dreams, Joseph was not aware of their greater significance or of the immense suffering implied in their fulfillment. He scarcely believed in them beyond the wishfulness of his strange personality. The greater destiny of his family, his people, and the world were hidden from view.

All his life, he continued to dream. Dreaming became the dominant motif of his actions. What was at first imagination and the visions of a spoiled youth became a tremendous and intricate framework of reality. He became so dominated by the dream that he hesitated to digress from it. He did not even send a letter home saying, "I am here." Even when he was the master of Egypt, he feared lest he do the wrong thing and disturb the working out of the dream. He had a certain dread of interfering with the unreal fabric of the apparition. From being a dreamer of dreams, Joseph became the person of the dream. He developed from reverie and conceit and ignorance of the dream's meaning, to a man who experienced the dream, no longer as wish fulfillment, but as a burden and a responsibility and a course of action from which there could be no digression. Joseph grew into something of a prophet then, except that he was never, to the last moment, quite certain and hence fell short of prophecy and remained Joseph, the eternal dreamer.

When he questioned his brothers at the end of a maze of complications that he had himself created, he asked, "Doth my father yet live?" (Genesis 45:3). He feared that there might be some deception, on the part either of his brothers or of the dream. If he could not meet his father alive, the dream would not be fulfilled. Thus when he heard that his father lived, he understood that the whole vision would be realized and that he could at last know redemption and release. He had come to the end of his dream. It had been all one dream, after all. True, there had been other dreamers and sleep visions in which he had taken part, but all the time he had been living out the substance of that single dream of his youth.

Like prophecy, the dream also needs someone who will embody it and give it reality by making events fit the scheme of vision. In embodying his dream, clinging to the inner insight and bending reality to it, Joseph completed the circle of a profound life experience—living out the dream.

9

Aaron

THE PEOPLE'S PROPHET

t is customary to speak of Moses and
Aaron together as the pair of redeemers who brought Israel forth from
bondage in Egypt. In the Bible story
itself, however, the figure of Moses is
dominant. From the Book of Exodus to the last
page of the Pentateuch, Moses is connected with
almost every phase of development: it is he who
is the hero of the Exodus and the Torah. His
brother, Aaron, appears as a secondary character,
sometimes even less than that. At the same time,
it is to be borne in mind that, historically, Aaron
has had a more extended influence than his illustrious brother.

Moses was a great personality in himself, a
special and unique phenomenon, with no equal

Exodus 4:14-16, 4:27-31, 6:13-9:12, 17:8-13, and 32:1-
35.

or parallel. Israel has never tried to raise another Moses from its midst—even though great sages used to be called "like a Moses," and in ancient synagogues there used to be a special seat, the chair of Moses, in which the rabbi sat. Moses was considered the father of the prophets, of those who preceded him and those who came after him. Nevertheless, all of these notions were metaphorical: there can be no real replica or imitation of Moses. Even his sons remain the stuff of legends.

Aaron, on the other hand, was the head of a line, father of a long succession of priests, who were called the sons of Aaron and constitute a vital part of the Jewish people for all time. When the Holy Temple still stood, the priests were certainly the core of the nation. But even afterward the tribe of priests stood apart from the others and were actively engaged in the spiritual and intellectual life of the people to a degree disproportionate to their numbers. The sons of Moses vanished from sight; the sons of Aaron became a permanent feature of national existence. From this point of view, the contribution of Moses as a leader may have been inestimably great and world shaking. But the one who remained as a living influence for generation upon generation was Aaron, the lesser of the pair of redeemers.

The endeavor to penetrate the character and personality of Aaron is thus far more complex than with any ordinary secondary biblical figure.

After all, he is an archetype, a model of priests for all generations. The chief ideal of priests in Israel, during and after the Temple period, was to be a disciple of Aaron and to maintain the tradition he established. Consequently, as high priest or as head of the priesthood, Aaron acquired many accomplishments and noble virtues deserving the adulation of the keepers of the sacred rituals. Much of it was founded in reality. On the Day of Atonement (Yom Kippur), a hymn is still recited about the glory of the priest, a hymn full of praise and veneration and based on a passage from the Book of Ben-Sira (Ecclesiasticus), concerning a real high priest who was a contemporary of his. Even more significant is the sentence in the Book of Malachi: "For the priest's lips should keep knowledge, and they should seek the law at his mouth: for he is the messenger of the Lord of Hosts" (2:7). The priest thus became the symbol of one who "loves peace and pursues peace, who loves people and brings them to the Torah," a teacher of the common folk, a guide and support. In short, the priest was not merely a functionary who performed rituals; he was a teacher of the people and had a broad and vital part to play in the community. And this archetypal image was established by Aaron.

The Bible portrait itself, aside from the legendary additions of later generations, is revealing. Nevertheless, the insights of the accumulated literature help us to discern the complementary relationship between Moses and Aaron. For instance, in the many allegorical descriptions of Israel as the bride and God as the bridegroom, with the Revelation at Mount Sinai as the wedding, Aaron is the one who gives the bride away, while Moses is the one who leads the groom to the wedding canopy.

Moses and Aaron represent two kinds of leader. The difference between them only reinforced the bond, cemented an alliance and a lasting friendship. At the same time, Moses never could descend altogether from the higher sphere; he did not even try to be liked or understood by the people. His whole essence, from the start of his career, was one of aloofness, almost that of the stranger or the one who comes from above. As the Torah commentator Avraham ben Ezra put it, "It was decreed in heaven that Moses should grow up in the royal household so that he could appear to the people as a king."

Aaron, however, was not only the assistant or the translator. True, he did provide Moses with help and support, but was also a leader in his own right, as is apparent from any scrupulous reading of the text. He was the popular chief, one of the tribe, a Levite, and a spokesman. Because he understood the people and sympathized with their shortcomings, he could guide them toward a goal that Moses had reached in a different way. Moses operated from the higher to the lower: he was the authority figure, giving orders and hardly ever explaining or educating. Aaron, on the other hand, functioned from the lower to the higher, trying to lead the people carefully, teaching and guiding them.

This difference between the two approaches may shed some light on the shameful episode of the Golden Calf. In this incident, Aaron cooperated with the sinners and even fashioned the Golden Calf—the worst failure of his career. One may, however, regard the matter in another light, recalling that, even in the Bible account, Aaron was put into a painful situation not unlike the one encountered by Moses later when he came down from the mountain. The main difference between them is that Moses had clear authority from above and could destroy the Golden Calf, overawe the main culprits, and even kill many of them. Aaron could do none of these things; he had no such authority from above. His authority came from below, from the people; and he was compelled to do their bidding. What he endeavored to do in this predicament was to raise popular sentiment into something more subtle and noble and more in keeping with his own concepts. When he agreed to cooperate in the casting of the Golden Calf, he was undoubtedly proceeding along his own mode of leadership—given to compromise and acquiescence—with the accompanying perils of "distorting the truth for the sake of peace."

So was the pattern of Aaron's personality fixed for the ages: "One who lives peace and pursues peace, loves the people and brings them to the Torah." There are many legends, in various sources, that describe him as trying to make peace between parties and people, using all possible means—whether legal or underhand, fair or unfair—all in order to achieve the most desirable of ends, "harmony between man and his neighbor, between man and wife."

The role of popular leader also imposed on Aaron the responsibility of acting as intermediary between the people and God. And later this responsibility did become the outstanding function of his sons, the priests. But in Aaron himself it was an intrinsic aspect of his personality: that is to say, he was both a vehicle of the people's will and able to draw from Moses something of the special authority and power from above. It is this aspect that makes him a messenger of God, a priest of the Lord. Hence, the eternal dual task of the priest: to serve as functionary in the Temple, manifesting and expressing the Holy to the people; and to serve as intermediary for the people before God.

Essentially, then, Aaron was a beloved man of the people. As the sages have pointed out, there is a significant but subtle difference in the way the nation mourned for each of this pair of redeemers. Concerning Aaron, it is written: "And when all the congregation saw that Aaron was dead, they mourned for Aaron thirty days, even all the house of Israel" (Numbers 20:29), whereas concerning the death of Moses, it is written: "And the children of Israel wept for Moses in the lowlands of Moab thirty days" (Deuteronomy 34:8). In other words, the mourning for Moses was a national, official ceremony; the mourning for Aaron was an expression of grief by all the houses and persons of Israel, big and small, men and women, each one being bound up in a specific way with the personality of Aaron.

To be sure, Aaron was more than just a popular leader close to the hearts of the folk; he was also a prophet—and he was a prophet even before Moses became one. He was the prophet of the Children of Israel in Egypt and, in this sense, created the background and the basis for the people's later acceptance of the priestly élite. For many generations, the priest dealt with more than the ceremonial functions of religion: he was judge, teacher, guide. True, the priestly tasks listed in the Book of Malachi are specified in the Torah itself, but they are more in the nature of peripheral comments. The clear image of what the priest should be was, for all time, the example set by the specific personality of Aaron, the son of Amram.

Of course, one may also remember the short-comings and failures of the man: the ignominious affair of the Golden Calf; the offensive, evil talk with his sister Miriam, against Moses, their brother. Both these incidents only confirm the view of Aaron as a man of the people—a priest, but not a holy man. He was not a man from another realm, from somewhere else. He did not even pretend to have come from beyond Israel; and, in spite of his splendid attire as high priest and the grandeur of his function, Aaron remained an integral part of the tribal culture. In fact, the closer the bond between priest and people, the stronger the position of the priestly class.

It is likely that the most magnificent period of the priests was in the time of the Second Temple. During the period of the First Temple, the functionaries in the Holy Temple always had to have the support of royal authority, and their power and glory were connected with that of the house of David, whereas, during the first half of the period of the Second Temple, the actual political sovereignty of the nation and all the real power lay with the high priest. And even afterward, when the secular kingdom was established, it was the priestly family of the Hasmoneans who held the power. Although the Maccabees were not of the highest rank, the fact that they were of the hereditary priesthood carried considerable weight. It expressed the warm and vital relation between the people of Israel and the class of priests. Even the rise and eventual fall of this consecrated aristocracy was connected with the fact that they were closely involved with the various currents and forces operating among the common people.

What is important for an understanding of the personality of Aaron is the undiminished vitality of the connection he established with all the various sections of the nation. Always the angel-messengers of God and the human teacher-guides of men, the priests filled the role of Aaron for centuries. And whenever the high priest forgot that he was not only the emissary of God but also the liaison with the Children of Israel, there was a crisis, in the priesthood as well as in the nation— a crisis that was usually decried as a repudiation of the true role of the sons of Aaron.

Hence, when, in the course of history, a priest ceased to be a true disciple of Aaron and concentrated on remaining only a biological heir, he ceased to be a leader in Israel. Even though he continued to be a member of the tribe of priests and Levites and played his role in the holy service, once the example and tradition set by Aaron was severed, the priest lost his place as a leader of the community. Those leaders who did arise in time were men who followed the way of Aaron, whether they were his direct descendants or came from other tribes of Israel.

10

Miriam

THE BIG SISTER

he Exodus from Egypt was marked by the leadership of the three children of Amram—Moses, Aaron, and Miriam, and wherever they are mentioned in the Bible or in the writings of the sages, there is a tendency to refer to them as one unit. Different as they were in character, personality, and role, the three are inextricably bound together in a way that exceeds the ties of family or generation. For example, tradition maintains that all three died "by the mouth of God," even though Scripture only describes Aaron's death in this way.

Each of the three leaders had a particular role to play in the redemption of Israel. In terms of their relationship to the people, Moses is not empowered by the people but is really a Divine

Exodus 2:1-9 and 15:20-21; Numbers 12:1-16.

emissary. Although he also intercedes with God on behalf of the nation, he is much more God's representative to the people than a popular national leader who rules through national consensus. Both Miriam and Aaron, on the other hand, are seen as the representatives of the nation, the redeemers acting from within. They were the leaders of the people in their Egyptian exile, rising from the ranks and preparing Israel to accept the prophecy of Moses. It is said in the Bible that Miriam and Aaron were prophets in their own right; that is, their vision was not dependent on that of Moses.

Miriam was the leader-prophet of the women of Israel, while Aaron was the leader of the men. This is evident after the crossing of the Red Sea, following the great song (Exodus 15) that Moses sang in honor of all Israel, when Miriam separately organized the women in response, with "timbrels and with dances" (Exodus 15:20). The role of a women's chorus is a common phenomenon in Middle Eastern culture and may be of even greater antiquity than the male chorus. As in the Song of Deborah, the singing of women, usually accompanied by timbrels and dancing, gave expression to war, battle, and miracle. Frequently the song was led by a solo singer, who would compose the litany as well as deliver it. The singer was, therefore, first and foremost a poetess, although occasionally she was also called upon to articulate and summarize a historical experience or to arouse the nation to cope with a present or forthcoming challenge. The Song of Miriam is the first instance of such a song in the Bible and thus indicates that she was not only the sister of Moses and of Aaron but also a leader in her own right.

The sages pointed out the special gifts associated with each of the redeemers on the journey to Canaan: manna with Moses, clouds of glory with Aaron, and the well with Miriam. Hence, the persistent tradition of the sages regarding "Miriam's well," which, according to the *Aggadah*, is a wandering well. In talmudic times, for instance, it was said that Miriam's well could be found in the Mediterranean Sea and seen from the heights of Mount Carmel. In other generations, it was said that the well was in the Sea of Galilee. Many commentaries and legends throughout history have told of striking Miriam's well as a source of water or as a miracle-working spring that appears as a fountain of healing and redemption and then vanishes.

Beyond the national role of Miriam and her place as a leader and a prophetess of her generation, she was primarily the sister of Aaron and, even more, of Moses. She was the "big sister" of the family and, as such, was naturally in charge of the younger children. In the biblical description of her family relations, one may perceive the attitude of the older sister and the feeling of responsibility toward her younger brothers. One senses it not only when the baby Moses was placed in the basket, but even over eighty years later, when Miriam and Aaron were speaking against Moses—and were rebuked by God for their arrogance (Numbers 12:1-14). Clearly, her meddling indicates that despite their advanced age, the older sister still felt responsible for her brother's physical and spiritual well-being—a not uncommon "big sister" phenomenon.

The biblical text does not provide us with much information about Miriam's personal life. We know little of her marriage, although it is clear that she was married, and we learn little about her offspring. Again, the knowledge we have is almost entirely from the aggadic tradition; and according to this source, Miriam was, to a greater or lesser degree, the maternal forebear of the King of Judah. Her husband was of the tribe of Judah, and her descendants established the leading families from which David was ultimately descended. According to this same tradition, Moses, Aaron, and Miriam bear the three crowns with which Israel is blessed: the crown of prophecy, which is Moses' (in the words of Maimonides, Moses is the father of prophets); the crown of priesthood, which is Aaron's; and the crown of kingship, which is Miriam's. It is held that Bezalel, the builder of the Sanctuary (Exodus 37:1), was one of Miriam's descendants, and that Hur, the enigmatic man who stood at Moses' side during the battle against Amalek (17:9-16), may have been her son. All this exemplifies the close bond between the leaders of the tribe of Judah and the family of Amram. Aaron's wife, for example, was the daughter of the head of the tribe of Judah at that time.

However, despite her other important ties, Miriam is first and foremost the guardian of Moses. The Talmud relates that Miriam prophesied to her parents that they would bear a son who would be the redeemer of Israel. Miriam standing "afar off" (Exodus 2:4) to watch what fate would befall the baby Moses was therefore attempting to verify her own prophecy. That is to say, Miriam felt responsible for Moses not only as a sister in the family sense, but in the more important role as herald of his coming.

This role of harbinger of redemption is a repeated theme. Tradition has it that Elijah the Prophet would be the forerunner of the Messiah-Redeemer and identifies him with Pinhas the Priest. The Talmud explores the relationship between the Messiah and the Book of Zechariah's "righteous priest." (This relationship can also be seen, from a very different angle, in the Dead Sea Scrolls.) Elijah-Pinhas, the righteous priest, was the precursor of the Messiah; and the three children of Amram are, each in his own way, redeemers and forerunners of the ultimate redeemer.

During the Exodus from Egypt, the theme of the double herald is expressed in the division of roles between Aaron and Miriam. The tidings of redemption have two distinct aspects, paralleled in the tradition of Abraham and Sarah where "Abraham converts the men and Sarah converts the women." More than once, the sages have pointed out that, in almost everything concerning the Exodus from Egypt, it is the men who seem to follow after the women, both in leaving Egypt and in receiving and submitting to the Law. This recognition of the special role of women in Exodus in stimulating and inspiring the men appears in several places in the Midrash. Indeed, because the women did not participate in the sin of the Golden Calf, they were accorded their own festival—the New Moon—which was not celebrated by men. For many generations women abstained from work on the New Moon, and, in some communities, the tradition continues to this day, at least in regard to certain labor. This tradition is also related to the fact that, like the moon, women have a physical monthly cycle, experiencing a monthly renewal.

According to this concept, Miriam is the first herald of redemption and hence her role in guarding Moses in the basket. Not only did she physically protect it from danger, but she also stood "afar off, to know what would be done to him" (Exodus 2:4) because her role was that of guarding the vision of what was to be. She took upon herself the role of herald and, more than this, the role of ensuring that the tidings were fulfilled.

Redemption is often a stormy, revolutionary process and usually a threatening and dangerous one. In order for an individual or a nation to be redeemed, there must be preparation; the ground-work must be established. Redemption has no significance for one who is unprepared for it. To be redeemed from Egypt, the people of Israel had to pass through several stages of spiritual prepa-ration in order to become willing to leave. It was not enough to suffer torments, since the bitter-ness of Israel alone could not suffice as an instru-ment of redemption; a framework of expectation must ensure that future greatness could be ac-cepted. Many commentators claim that Miriam's name* is symbolic and expresses the bitterness of Israel's life in Egypt. Be that as it may, her role in the decisive situation where Moses was discov-ered by Pharaoh's daughter was to ensure that the redeemer was not lost, that the dual relationship with the people would be kept: he would, on the one hand, be in the king's house and, on the other, remain bound to his people and to his birth.

This part of the story symbolizes the essence of Miriam's role as the older sister, not only of Moses and Aaron but, in a sense, of the whole

---

*In Hebrew, *mar* is "bitter."

nation. She was not the mother of redemption, but she made redemption possible. Her task was to know the priorities, to recognize the things that must be protected and preserved and to act accordingly. Later came also the ability to direct and control events and situations, to combine things correctly. These combinations were possibly not decisive in themselves, and events would perhaps have arranged themselves unaided. Only their impact, their course, and their interaction required Miriam's intervention to become significant.

In the Exodus from Egypt, it is most significant that it was forbidden, or impossible, to bring about redemption or revelation by force. At every stage, there must be acquiescence and deep faith. For this, the nation needed the very prophets who grew from its ranks, Aaron and Miriam, to prepare them for the redemption. Similarly, the people required preparation before experiencing the Revelation at Sinai. Without their first proclaiming "We shall do and we shall hear" (Exodus 24:7), there could have been no Revelation.

In the Bible, Yocheved was the mother of the redeemer, and Miriam was the one who helped redemption to be created. She was, as it were, the midwife, which is how her role is seen in the Midrash. The midwife does not herself create the child; the fetus is conceived by others. The midwife is essential to the process of birth; she sees the newborn safely into the world. One midrashic commentary identifies Shiphrah and Puah, the two Hebrew midwives (Exodus 1:15-21), with Yocheved and Miriam. Thus, the women who brought the children of the Hebrews into the world also prepared and created the conditions for their redemption.

The Exodus has been interpreted as a second chance for man and womankind: it is as though God were saying that, at the time of the sin of the Tree of Knowledge, the commandment to abstain from eating its fruit was given to Adam, and the sin was the sin of Eve, who did not herself receive the commandment. Therefore, in order to receive the Torah, and in a sense be created afresh, Israel must be approached from the opposite direction, through the women, *Bet Yaakov*, and thereafter to convince the men. This new combination of events and forces would be more stable because, despite all later errors and deviations, the role of *Bet Yaakov*, the women, in accepting the Torah with "We shall do and we shall hear" (Exodus 24:7), remains the significant and existential task of women throughout the generations. Herein, too, lies the essence of Miriam's role: she is the "big sister" who watches and worries and prepares for the future—an essential and fundamental part of the process of redemption.

11

Joshua

THE COMPLEMENTARY
DISCIPLE

oses and Joshua form an unusual combination, rare in Jewish history as well as in the records of humanity as a whole. It is the conjunction of a truly great teacher and a truly great disciple.

To be sure, the pairing of Moses and Joshua is not straightforward and simple. The relationship between them goes beyond that of master and pupil: the disciple was indisputably superior in at least one respect; and while the teacher was the sole creator of the theory and builder of the foundation, the pupil was the one who established it firmly and concluded the task. Joshua was, therefore, more than a model disciple and a faithful follower; he was a personality in himself. In this sense, Moses is one of the few great leaders who

---

Exodus 17:8-16; Numbers 11:28-29 and 27:15-23: Book of Joshua.

managed to find a disciple who would not only follow after him but complement his personality.

From this point of view, Joshua is not the fresh beginning of a new historical stage nor is he a whole character. Even though the scope of his actions is comparable to those of his teacher, he himself did not make the policy or plan the course of the larger strategy. His primary task was to execute the plan conceived by Moses.

The sages have said that were it not for the sins of Israel, many of the books of the Bible would never have been written. The books of the prophets, for instance, are almost entirely devoted to descriptions of the sins of Israel, the punishments that would be meted out to its people, and each prophet's own words of admonition. But for its sins, the only books that would have been given to Israel were the five books of the Torah (Pentateuch) and the Book of Joshua, which, within the framework of a certain historical view, belongs to the Torah. In many ways, and in contrast to customary usage, the Book of Joshua does not begin a new cycle of events but completes and rounds out the message of the Torah and, especially, of the Book of Deuteronomy. Many of the unsolved problems and unfulfilled promises left behind at the death of Moses were resolved by Joshua. It was after him that a new historical period set in—the post-Torah age, during which Israel remained alone, without direct guidance from above.

In the inwardness of his leadership, Joshua reminds one of Moses. Joshua was not a leader who functioned according to some occasional prophetic message that came to him from time to time, nor was he a leader who relied on himself, like Samuel or, by contrast, like David. Joshua's effectiveness as military commander, statesman, or religious authority stemmed from the constant guidance he received from a higher power. At any critical moment, before any important move, he received from above instruction on how to act—and, in this respect, he was like Moses. He pursued a course of leadership that was begun without his participation or comprehension. As a private person, he might have been able to introduce minor variations in this plan; but, ultimately, his task was to bring to a decisive conclusion in history—through conquest and settlement—the great plan of the Exodus. Only by his actions was the Exodus fulfilled. Moses was the chief figure of the historical evacuation from Egypt, but the completion of this task was accomplished by Joshua.

This view of Joshua's role has been shared by many commentators of previous generations in their remarks concerning the (seemingly mistaken) prophecy of Moses: "For I know that after my death ye shall utterly corrupt yourselves and turn aside from the way which I have commanded you" (Deuteronomy 31:29). These commentators

maintained that this prophecy was not quite fulfilled, because, under the leadership of Joshua, the
people did continue to keep the commandments
of the Torah. However, the sages continued, the
disciple might be considered like the master, as
an extension of his essence: thus, as long as
Joshua lived, it might be said that Moses lived in
him. And, therefore, the era of Moses may be seen
as having ended with the death of Joshua and not
with the death of Moses. It is only with the passing of Joshua that the period of the Exodus came
to an end, and a new historical era began for the
Jewish people. This new era can be seen as the
history of Israel on its own, grappling by itself
with the intrinsic conflicts of nationhood.

In several ways, then, Moses and Joshua were
part of the same initial wave or thrust—but the
differences between them were far-reaching. The
most conspicuous dissimilarity is the fact that
Joshua was not the originator of policy and events;
he was the one who carried out the orders. As the
sages put it, "The face of Moses is like the sun,
the face of Joshua like the moon" (*Baba Batra* 75a).
Thus, the greatness of the two is depicted in contrast to all the other lights that followed after them;
but at the same time, there is the distinct insinu-
ation that, whereas the one is the great source of
light, the other is but a reflection—even if both
illuminate brightly and spread the word of God
in the world. Moses spoke with God directly, face

to face, while Joshua spoke to God as a man or, rather, as a prophet.

Another *midrash* (biblical commentary or explanation) expounds on the difference between Moses and Joshua by pointing to the incident, just before the conquest of Jericho, when Joshua bowed to the Lord of Hosts. As usual, the *midrash* relates to the spirit of the biblical account rather than to the explicit narrative and, in this instance, tells how the angel, military commander of the Hosts of Heaven, pleaded with Joshua, saying, "When Moses was alive, he did not want to see me, but now, at least you can receive me so that I can help the people of Israel." And the situation is easily understood when one remembers that Moses was himself of the order of an angel of God, appearing thus before the people and, as such, in no need of another angelic messenger, while Joshua did need such assistance from above. All of which brings us back to the connection between the face of the sun and the face of the moon.

Nevertheless, the difference between Moses and Joshua is not entirely resolved by the words of the sages. There is more here than a confrontation between greater and smaller or between a creative, original person and a relatively minor adapter. Joshua displayed certain traits that not only were unique and original but, what is more, were not to be found in Moses. Hence, Moses' need of Joshua—as was made apparent in the surprising way Moses spoke to Joshua on the eve of the first battle with Amalek at Refidim.

Before Moses climbed the hill in order to stand there and pray with outstretched hands, he said to Joshua, "Choose us men and go forth and fight with Amalek tomorrow" (Exodus 17:8). At this time, just after the departure from Egypt, Joshua was still a very young man, and this is the first time he is mentioned in the Bible. We know very little about his personality, his family, his origins, even though there are some vague hints. The point is that Moses spoke to this unknown youngster almost as to an equal: "Choose us men and go forth and fight." These words seem to confirm that Moses was fully cognizant of his own limitations: he knew that he was and would always remain a "man of God," even though he descended occasionally (sometimes successfully) to the world of men and deeds.

Ultimately, Moses was not the man of action or the practical thinker. In order to get to the people, he had to be helped by someone who had a nearer relationship to them. The enormous spiritual gap between Moses and the nation limited his ability to lead them. Moses understood the people from within himself, unto the utmost degree of self-sacrifice and love; but he was above and beyond them. He led them and had no other concern than their welfare, but he could not relate seriously to their problems and requests. He even complained,

"Have I conceived this people . . . that thou shouldst say unto me, 'Carry them in thy bosom, as a nursing father beareth the sucking child'" (Numbers 11:12). That is, he could not see the people as adults; instead, he placed himself in the role of someone taking care of crying and dirty infants, who are incapable of gratitude or comprehension.

At the same time, he was fully aware of the need to be in direct touch with the people and their problems. This contact was made at a certain time and was formalized in the priesthood, through his brother Aaron, a man of the folk.

But the person who could transform the vision and the prophetic message into practical reality, who could give body to the spirit, was Joshua. In this sense, Joshua was not a copy or an extension of Moses; he was the complement of the personality of Moses.

Among the tasks given to Joshua was leading the people into the Land of Israel, whereas Moses was prohibited from setting foot in the Promised Land. This prohibition, which is a matter of concern to all who read the Bible seriously, is in a way connected with the essential personalities involved. Moses was the spiritual man, the one connected with the manna from heaven, with the pillar of fire, and with all that was beyond the ordinary laws of physical nature. But the Land of Israel was definitely a physical place; and, therefore, the physical fulfillment of the Torah was the task of someone else. The Torah of Moses and the personality of Moses were, in a certain way, beyond this world. In order to effect a transformation of this transcendent Torah, to bring the prophetic message back to the realm of the physical where man can receive it, an adequate vehicle, a Joshua, was required.

This relationship between Moses and Joshua is a refrain that is reflected also in the encounters between them. In the war with Amalek, Moses stood on the hill to pray, while Joshua went out to fight. In the revelation of the Torah at Mount Sinai, Joshua stayed at his post, while Moses went up to the top, to the mist and the clouds where God was. Aaron and Hur remained with the people, while Joshua remained alone on the mountain. He, Joshua, did not belong to the people; he was far above them. At the same time, he was not Moses; he was somewhere in between. When Moses descended from the summit, the first—and, indeed, the only other—person to see the unbroken tablets of the Covenant was Joshua, the one who accompanied him and eventually brought about the realization of Moses' wishes.

Also in the conversations between them, there was a curious intimacy, in spite of the fact that they were not kinsmen. Moses talked to him almost like a son, while Joshua reciprocated with the love and zeal reserved for a father. When Eldad and

Medad presumed to prophesy without the special permission of Moses, the first reaction of Joshua was: "My lord, Moses—destroy them!" (Numbers 11:28). In short, Joshua was saying—in a spontaneous outburst of jealous solicitude for the honor and greatness of Moses—How dare anyone raise his voice in divine prophecy except you? As for the response of Moses, one may discern a certain delicate humor and affection: "Art thou jealous for my sake?" For Moses was well acquainted with the anxious zeal of those who love greatly.

It is clear, then, that Joshua was jealous for Moses' authority—how can there be any other prophet but Moses?—while Moses could say with broad tolerance, "Let all the people of God be prophets." In this conversation, Joshua also expressed the view of the practical man of action—the need for one leader and only one—while Moses, the visionary and thinker, could allow himself to be generous-minded.

The problem of the division between the authority of the priesthood and the authority of the leaders (such as the judges or the kings) would reappear in the history of Israel time and again. Joshua was confronted with it early in his career, when the Lord commanded Moses to take Joshua and give him his commission and set him before Eleazar, the priest, "who shall ask counsel for him after the judgment of Urim before the Lord" (Numbers 27:21). A pair of leaders were thus set up: Joshua and Eleazar, the priest, son of Aaron. In practice, this ideal of Moses of twin leadership did not materialize. Joshua clearly became the dominant of the pair, just as Moses and Aaron were never really equal.

Joshua was more pragmatic than his teacher, Moses. It was for this reason that he, rather than Moses, was the one to bring matters to their fulfillment in history. At the same time, Joshua was fully aware of his place, as the "servant of Moses," as the one who carried out Moses' injunctions. And when Joshua had finished the task imposed on him by Moses, he emphasized again and again that it was the completion of some grand scheme.

The parting assembly, at which Joshua articulated the completion of this task, is a rare phenomenon in history and is a striking reflection of the fateful period in the life of the nation. Joshua released the bonds of his central authority, disbanded the army that he himself had formed, and—in almost utopian fashion—proclaimed the end of the state: There was to be no more central government; every man could now decide for himself. He, Joshua, had finished his task and concluded an era in history. And, therefore, at this unusual assembly, he reviewed the history of the Jewish people and declared: Our fathers lived on the other side of the river; they worshiped other gods. Now—in the language of the legend—God has brought us to this land where we can worship

Him. The promise given to Moses and to the Children of Israel has been fulfilled, and freedom is granted to make the choice whether to worship other gods or the Lord God.

This baring of the issue shows that Joshua was well aware that his life's work had been a continuation and a completion, leading to a new start. He was the one who, in actual fact, brought about the concrete realization of the hopes and dreams of the patriarchs who founded the nation, as well as of Moses, who led its people out of Egypt.

From this point, Israel began to act on its own, to take responsibility for itself. With the passing of Joshua, the hero in the history of Israel was the nation itself. Joshua was well aware of the nature of his success in bringing the Exodus to a conclusion, but he made no attempt to create a dynasty of power for his family or those around him. In this last deed he showed how well he recognized the nature of the new era and his role in the Torah.

12

Deborah

THE POLITICAL PROPHETESS

Among the several prophetesses portrayed in the Bible, the most complete and detailed picture is that of Deborah, who was also a judge in Israel. From the outset, this fact sets Deborah apart, since we can safely assume that, in those times—and, indeed, for many generations thereafter—the holders of such offices were men.

As the sages have said, it is almost certain that Deborah's role as judge was secondary to her role as prophetess. She became a judge because she was a prophetess, and not the contrary. In this sense she parallels the last of the judges, Samuel, who was fundamentally a prophet and, as a result, became a leader of the nation, in war and in peace.

Judges 4, 5.

Deborah is outstanding among the biblical prophetesses and differs substantially from the standard figure of the female seer in the ancient world. Prophetic powers were usually associated with virgins whose domain was that of augury and magic. The women consecrated to prophecy were released from the yoke of daily life. They had to dwell apart, protected from the seductions and temptations of normal life, so that all their spiritual and bodily forces were turned inward to serve the single goal of developing their exceptional gift. To this day, as in ancient times, the concept of monasticism expresses this same notion.

Deborah, like the other biblical prophetesses Miriam and Huldah, was a married woman in the full sense of the word. This fact teaches us something of the Jewish attitude not only to prophetic women but to prophecy as a whole. In Judaism, prophecy is not perceived as the experience of the unusual individual, gifted with parapsychological powers or possessing extraordinary spiritual characteristics that can be developed only at the expense of other manifestations of personality. Rather, the prophet is seen as a perfect, whole person. Far from being an eccentric, outside the normal mode of understanding, he or she is an individual who has achieved a state of perfection in the overall experience of life.

From this point of view, the image of the prophetess as judge is instructive and significant. Prophecy is revealed when the prophet speaks God's word: that is to say, he is made an instrument of a higher force and, at the moment of revelation, cannot be as other men. Even when there are preparation and training for prophecy, this is not in itself a conscious process. Moreover, prophecy contains within itself a certain turbulence, a certain disintegration of personality that is confined to the actual moment of prophetic revelation and, at other times, does not require isolation from the world. Thus, Deborah, the prophetess, was also a judge, dealing with the day-to-day affairs of the people of Israel, just as she dealt with the daily affairs of her own family. In this sense, the figure of the prophetess corresponds to the description of the ideal woman. She was not removed from society but lived and worked within its sphere. As against this, the cloistered virgin, like Jephthah's daughter, was seen as suffering a punishment, a torture that had no like. According to several sources, her fate was to remain a virgin throughout life, a tragic destiny that she and the daughters of Israel have bemoaned throughout the generations.

Deborah's role was primarily that of prophetess, but she was also a judge both in times of peace and in times of war. In fact, as in the case of the other judges, her decisive historical role emerged against the backdrop of external events, particularly in time of war and conflict.

It is interesting to compare Deborah to a heroine of a different age and culture—the French Jeanne d'Arc (who may have been influenced by the figure of Deborah). The difference between the two is immediately striking. Deborah did not set out at the head of the army, nor did she feel any need to do so. She found a man suited to the task of military commander and not only gave him control over the armed forces but tried as much as possible to avoid any personal participation, even as an observer.

It is characteristic of Deborah that she penalized Barak for his request for her support by telling him that he would not strike the decisive blow, would not achieve the final victory—the killing of Sisera, the enemy leader. Instead, this deed would fall to the hand of a woman, Yael. This punishment reveals another side of the nature of Deborah: the acceptance of a certain division of roles between men and women. She saw it as a man's function to go to war, and she herself refused to go—not because of any tenderness of heart or squeamishness (Deborah's song is one of the most bloodthirsty in all the Bible), but because it was simply not her job to do so. Her task was to inspire, to prophesy, to judge. She did not hanker after the fame and glory of command. She saw Barak's attempt to draw her into war as a weakness on his part, and though the end would be victory, it would be a woman who would strike the decisive blow.

The Song of Deborah is one of the great and beautiful hymns of the Bible. It reveals, in its tones and accents, facets of her femininity, as in the emphatic self-appraisal of her personality and role. Although a prophetess, Deborah saw her own position clearly. When we compare her song to another great victory poem, Moses' song (Exodus 15), there is one striking difference, despite the poetic similarities: Moses does not mention himself, while in the Song of Deborah, the prophetess refers to herself several times: "Until I Deborah arose, arose a mother in Israel" (Judges 5:7). The sages have already commented that both Deborah and Huldah, in a later age, may have been exhibiting an arrogance unbecoming in a prophet.

It seems that Deborah could not refrain from stressing her own importance in this way. After all, she did not award herself laurels that did not belong to her, but mentioned herself in a totally legitimate and appropriate way; it was simply that she could not forget the personal aspect in the midst of the historic event. This characteristic is seen in another element in the Song of Deborah that is exceptional in biblical poetry—Deborah's reckoning with all those who took, or did not take, part in the war—and is very striking, especially if we compare it with other judges of the period. Jephthah, for instance, though spiritually and personally of lesser stature than Deborah, settled accounts with the tribes that did not support him, only when he was forced to do so (Judges 12:2), while Gideon did his best to include the tribes who did not participate in the war by making them feel that they, too, were important to the victory (8:2). He did take punitive action where necessary but did not proclaim it as dire disgrace. Deborah, in her song, made an exact settlement of account with everybody involved: she praised those who went off to war, and abused, sometimes in the harshest way, those tribes and clans that did not join the battle.

A "blacklist" of this kind is characteristic of and unique to the Song of Deborah. It is especially interesting if one considers it as a song following on an overwhelming victory, which radically changes the political situation and should be a moment of rejoicing rather than of settling old scores.

Another, markedly feminine aspect of the song is seen in its conclusion. There is here no description of the fallen, of bodies torn or mangled by war, but it is psychologically extremely cruel. Throughout the poem, although it is a song of victory, there are almost no details of war; they are swallowed up in a great epic about the supremacy of the Lord God of Israel. The exception to this rule is that passage relating to the mother of Sisera. This is explicitly the reckoning of one woman with another and may be compared with the reckoning of Samuel with the mother of Agag—an episode no less striking in its simplicity but quite lacking in ridicule and venom (1 Samuel 15:33). Deborah graphically depicted the expectation of Sisera's mother and her waiting, watching, and preparing for his victorious coming, not yet knowing of his death and downfall. Irony and harsh mockery are often to be found in prophecy, but usually in a straightforward and explicit way. Here we have not the bluntness of an ax but the fineness of a needle. There is no doubt that this piercing, stinging quality was characteristic of Deborah.

The content of prophecy is a matter of mission; its style and expression are dependent on the essence of the prophet himself. True prophecy is distinguished, among other things, by the fact that no two prophets prophesy in the same manner. The prophet is analogous to a musical instrument, which can play only when it is played upon and yet retains its characteristic tone. Thus, Deborah's prophecy and poetry, as genuine prophecies and visions, also express clearly her personality as a human being—a woman of greatness and exaltation, who expresses deep sensitivity for the sublime and is capable of depicting a panorama of Divine Sinai-like Revelation—yet a woman of self-importance who harbors personal grudges and has a need to caustically mock the enemy even after it has been vanquished. The Song of Deborah, however, not only teaches us about her personality but gives us some insight into the significance of her actions and their importance.

The narrative of Deborah's story does not give a clear indication of her tribal affiliation, or of where she resided and in whose tribal territory she was active. In spite of this obscurity, it is relatively certain that she can be placed somewhere in the tribe of Ephraim, a point that significantly illuminates Deborah's actions and gives more weight to the historical implications of her war initiative. It becomes clear from her song that her description of herself as a "mother in Israel," the charismatic leader with great vision, was justified— even if it was perhaps inappropriate for her to say so herself. Her leadership had an added dimension of political significance that perhaps entitled her to make this great claim.

Most of the judges operated within the territory of one or two of the tribes, and the wars they led were primarily defensive—attempts to repel threats from outside the borders of the country. A given tribe would attend only to the security problems of its own bit of coastline, while another would simply enjoy the relative tranquillity of the moment. Deborah was exceptional in that her leadership, in war and peace, embraced practically all the tribes of Israel. She tried to form a broad alliance for a far-reaching national purpose that was as much political as military, even if not all the tribes cooperated in this alliance but, following old custom, did not see themselves obliged to enter a war not specifically theirs.

Deborah's initiative was an immense undertaking, akin to that of the original conquest of the land by Joshua and, in a sense, a continuation of it. Yakhin, king of Hatzor, not a new enemy of Israel, was vanquished and, with him, the Canaanite strength in the north was broken. The Canaanites, while not entirely destroyed, thenceforth disappeared as a political force from that area of the country.

Both the initiative for war and the gathering of many tribes under one banner and the ensuing political network of intertribal cooperation were all the acts of Deborah. The enemy was troublesome chiefly to the northern tribes, and Deborah tried to remove a threat that was not aimed directly at her tribe but that, in the future, might threaten the whole nation. In this sense, she did something that was attempted only many generations later by the kings of Israel. Thus, Deborah is revealed as a great historical personality, much more than a local judge or leader. She saw events on a large scale, not as opportune coincidences caused by a known force. She fulfilled a role of great historical scope and, in so doing, not only justified her title of "mother in Israel" but also the description of her age as the "age of Deborah." She left her mark on an era.

13

Samson

THE PROPHET OF POWER

n the Book of Judges, the central figures are described in a variety of ways. Some of the judges are portrayed in great detail. Others are so undefined that practically all we know of them is their names: for instance, Shamgar, son of Anath, who is mentioned in only two fragmented passages (Judges 3:31); or Ibzan of Bethlehem (12:8). Where we are provided with more information, the lines of description of these judges show surprising parallels, suited in fact to a certain type of revolutionary leader in other periods of history, and not only among the Jews.

First, none of the judges seem to have been conventionally accepted or officially declared leaders of the people or the tribe. They were individuals who achieved their positions of power

---

Judges 13-16.

from a secondary status or even less. They were the offspring of small, undistinguished families, decent enough folk, but not part of the ruling élite. They all had an unusual, charismatic personality, by means of which they managed to emerge from their social limitations and bring some sort of salvation to their nation or tribe. They were able to show their gifts as military leaders in time of war, bringing victory and then putting the state in order and providing it with a period of stability and rest.

If we compare these judges, in terms of situation, with figures from other nations—like those of the French Revolution, the American Revolution, the Civil War in England, and the like—we shall discover them to be, for the most part, of the same human type: of undistinguished extraction, but possessing military gifts and powers of administration and leadership that made them saviors at a time of national crisis. The national crisis is the factor that conspicuously emphasizes the inability of the existing establishment to govern and impels the rise of a new leadership. Ethniel, son of Kenaz, was the younger brother, probably a stepbrother, of Caleb, the leader of the tribe. So, too, the origins of Ehud, son of Gera, and Jephthah, the Gileadite, were not in the existing upper crust of society (Judges 2,3,11).

The judges, then, were mainly of more or less obscure birth, and their strong personalities fit a certain pattern of historic significance. The one exception is Samson. One would find it impossible to fit him into the social and personal pattern of the judges. Indeed, he does not readily fit into any category of heroes in Israel. The ways in which the personality of Samson differs from the other great leaders in the Bible are many and varied. To begin with, he was hardly much of a "judge" or chief of the people. If a leader, he was one from a distance. Almost everything he did was as a private individual. The exploits of Samson were his own heroic deeds; they belonged to him alone as an individual. The passage in the testimony of Jacob that was considered a prophecy about Samson, "Dan shall be a serpent by the way, an adder in the path, that biteth the horse's heels so that his rider shall fall backward" (Genesis 59:17), has been interpreted as meaning that just as snakes and adders always act alone, and not in groups, so did Samson function as a leader without any followers.

It may well be that, as a result of his actions, new political configurations were formed and the balance of power shifted. In whatever fashion his actions may have influenced others, ultimately he was a loner, a man who performed great deeds on his own, by himself. In this respect, he is exceptional in the annals of the judges and other great leaders of Israel. The Book of Judges always describes the individual leader within the body of the people, as a part of the national history. His importance lay in his power to draw others to him; in an hour of emergency, he called and gathered the clan around him. Samson, however, did not call anyone to help him. At the most, he would ask his relatives of the tribe of Judah not to interfere too much—and that is about as much as he had to do with the nation or any part of it, whether of his own or any other tribe. In short, among all the personalities in Jewish history whose actions have been of national significance, Samson is outstanding in his solitariness, in his acting alone.

As may be surmised, the man himself was a mass of interesting contradictions and hidden potential. Born out of an extraordinary prophecy— in which an angel revealed himself to his parents and predicted Samson's birth—his whole early life and education were exceptional. Apart from Isaac, the Hebrew Bible has no other story of such an eminent birth, foretold by an angel; even Moses, Samuel, David, and other great figures were not announced in this way to their parents. Nor were any of these parents given instructions on how to educate their child. Samson, however, who was born as the fulfillment of a promise, was raised in terms of the revelation about him: "The child shall be a Nazarite to God from the womb to the day of his death" (Judges 13:7). From this one might have expected the boy to have grown into a holy man, a person of outstanding moral stature and prophetic wisdom.

As the youth matured, however, he not only failed to be a holy prophet but did not even fit the pattern of judge. Indeed, as far as we know, the judges and the great leaders of that age and later were disciplined and decent men, whose private lives were for the most part beyond reproach. The type conforms, as stated, to parallel figures of the great revolutionary leaders of other nations—men who were generally upright, God-fearing examples to others, were identified with the national struggle, and inspired great respect among their contemporaries. Samson thus offers us a rather perplexing exception to the rule—appearing to be mischievous, vehement, full of a certain devil-may-care impetuosity and bravado.

Even Jephthah, the Gileadite—of questionable extraction and breeding—when he became a judge, took his task seriously and carried it out with propriety and responsibility (Judges 11). Samson, by contrast, used his great strength for purposes that may have had national importance, but he seemed like something of an adolescent ruffian. In this respect, he is exceptional in Jewish history. We do not encounter a real national leader in this mold even among other nations. He is reminiscent of the mythical Hercules who, out of an excess of strength, vitality, and wild instincts, is not entirely responsible for his actions.

Even without the supernatural and angelic framework of Samson's birth, his contradictory personality would have been disturbingly out of place in the biblical context. The special circumstances of his birth only add to our perplexity about his being a Nazarite, and altogether make us wonder why so much space was allotted to him in the Scriptures. What, after all, does he express? Many other noble heroes and events are barely mentioned by name: for instance, Shamgar, son of Anath, who killed six hundred men, or the valiant officers who fought with David.

Thus, solving the riddle of Samson's personality may help us understand something fundamental about the Bible and could provide an invaluable clue to the inner meaning of heroic action as a mode of revelation.

First, however, it would be appropriate to examine more closely the phenomenon of prophecy. A prophet, in the biblical sense, is someone who, by virtue of his personal characteristics and of his having been chosen by God—as in the case of Jeremiah, "Before I formed thee in the belly I knew thee" (1:5)—becomes a vessel for what the medieval sages called the Divine Plenty. The resultant prophecy is the action of this plenty on the chosen individual, who has thereby been fashioned into a vehicle of expression of divine speech. When the person is thus functioning, his humanity is held in abeyance; he is the instrument of something far greater than his human capacities. As a prophet, the speech that issues from him contains the higher wisdom; it expresses the omen and the vision. Moreover, not only is the content of the prophecy of utmost significance, but so also is the way the prophecy is manifested in the prophet and the prophet himself. Revelation is coming through the prophet; the Divine Plenty is descending upon the human race.

The incalculable importance of the phenomenon goes beyond the specific message; it is a point of contact between the higher and the lower worlds, showing us that they are not separate. Through the existential power of his experience, the prophet proves that there is a channel of communication with worlds ordinarily out of our reach. This is what the prophet is charged with, and this is what sanctifies all that he does.

This phenomenon of the higher power streaming through a member of the human race can manifest itself in other forms. True, the classical expression is that of divine speech in the throat of the prophet; but the *Shekhinah* can manifest itself also in the hands of the chosen one. Thus, the purpose of the whole story of Samson may be to show us this other aspect of divine manifestation. And indeed, though Samson was a paradoxical and unconventional sort of prophet, there is no denying that the Divine Plenty flowed through him. To be sure, most of the prophets who have come to deliver a message to humanity have expressed themselves in intellectual and even poetic terms, while Samson's vehicle of expression was through a superhuman strength, a physical prowess that so transcended the ordinary that it was obviously divine in origin.

This idea—which the sages considered, as in the Talmud, where it is said that five people were formed on a divine pattern, among them Samson—is mentioned plainly in the Bible text: "And the spirit of the Lord began to move him at times in the camp of Dan between Zorah and Eshtaol" (Judges 13:25). What was this spirit that moved him? The Midrash claims that it was the spirit of strength from God. And if so, the spirit of God, which in other prophets appeared as words of wisdom and righteousness, appeared in Samson as an enormous strength. He is, therefore, the prophet of divine power expressed as physical force. His whole personality is a vehicle of this aspect of the Divine, as is pointed out several times in the story. He himself told it to Delilah in the innocence of his heart, when he tried to hint to her what would make him like other men.

There is a curious version here of the problem of the prophet who would like to flee from his prophecy and be like everyone else. And, of course, all the things Samson contrived did not make much sense and had nothing to do with the source of his strength.

When, however, he ceased to be a Nazarite and relinquished his hold on the "prophetic contact," severing the special bond between himself as a man and himself as a vehicle of power from above, he became like other men. Samson was not a hero because of his greater muscular strength: in fact, he was always surprising the people around him, the Philistines, the women, and so on. He does not seem to have been an exceptionally big or impressively muscular man. His strength derived from something within him that functioned on a different level. In other words, he was a channel of divine manifestation, even if in a manner unique and unfamiliar to us. And because he was a genuine prophet, the few prayers he uttered were answered at once. There is the instance at Lehi, when he was thirsty after smiting his enemies with the jawbone of an ass, and water came for him to drink; and the time he stood between the pillars of the great house and asked to "die with the Philistines" (Judges 16:30). The point is that his requests were not concerned with the future of the nation, nor did he ask for wisdom for himself or a holy temple for the people. He asked for strength because he was that sort of a prophet. And he was a true prophet in that he was a vehicle of divine might.

The whole story of Samson, then, confirms the biblical principle that all the positive powers in the world, no matter in what form or category, come from the single divine power. As it is written: "Let not the wise man glory in his wisdom, neither let the mighty man glory in his might, let not the rich man glory in his riches: But let him that glorieth glory in this, that he understandeth and knoweth Me" (Jeremiah 9:23-24). The wise man glorying in his wisdom is the one who relies on his cleverness, who pretends to know it all, the politician who stands against the prophet, while the prophet is like a "child" receiving his inspiration from a higher wisdom. The figure of Samson expresses the idea of someone being chosen to function as an instrument of the Divine without the use of words. This is what makes him unique among the prophets of the Bible, who are for the most part prophets of wisdom or at least of wisdom of the heart.

The manifestation of Divine Plenty in Samson is perhaps paralleled only in the vision of the Messiah—the one who will be a direct instrument of divine power and of immense capacity for action. When Samson was inspired, he became a different man. In himself, he may well have been a simple person, quite unaware of the larger significance of his deeds. But since his prophecy was not that of words but of great strength—of someone who can lift the gates of Gaza and walk away with them, who can tear the lion and topple the pillars of a palace—he did not have to say anything. These actions were the expressions of God within him, manifestations of a superhuman strength that came from above.

14

Ruth

THE HIDDEN SPRING

R uth is one of the two women in the Bible for whom a whole book is named. She is also the one woman in the Scriptures who has no human fault ascribed to her: she stands alone not only among the heroines of the Bible but among most of the men. Although Ruth's early life was neither easy nor simple, and certainly unsatisfying in many ways, its defects were foisted upon her from without while she maintained her wholeness and purity of being.

We have no real information regarding Ruth's origins. The tradition of the sages is that she was a princess, a daughter of Eglon, King of Moab. Be that as it may, in the biblical story, Ruth is not seen as being rooted in her own nation or as being essentially part of her own people. Rather, she

---

Book of Ruth; see also Genesis 19:30–38.

appears from the very beginning to be out of place. Thus, she has become the archetype of the convert, reinforcing the view that converts do not really undergo any substantial process of change, of passing from one essential state to another. They do not undergo a process of renewal or re-birth but are people who have belonged to another world without knowing it. Like Ruth, they are people who find themselves.

In a larger context, the story of Ruth is an example of a process, a vast ordering of forces and events that extends throughout the Bible. It is a story in which people finally find their rightful place, and in which personal, family, and histori-cal connections finally come to fulfillment. It is not always clear how this happens, but at times an individual completes a certain picture, a his-torical cycle that had been unfolding for many generations.

The sages have already commented that Ruth perfected or, in other words, redeemed several figures from the distant past. Hence, her associa-tion with the kings of Moab, because, in the lan-guage of the Lurianic Kabbalah, she redeemed the holy spark of Moab. Here an ancient, forgotten link is once again revealed, and the concealed essence of Moab is made manifest.

According to the Book of Genesis, Moab was the son of Lot, the close relative of Abraham, not only his brother's son but perhaps also his brother-in-law. In a sense, Lot was Abraham's counterpart, his companion who endeavored to imitate him. The similarity between Abraham and Lot is, of course, only partial, because Lot had many failings, ending his life in a way that was both sad and unpleasant, and his heirs were children born of an incestuous relationship. Nevertheless, it is possible here to trace a continuous line. In another biblical story—the selling of Joseph—the same idea appears. In the Midrash, it is considered that, in this story, the different patterns of history with their many-sided events and actions, good and bad, are all strands that eventually "weave the light of the Messiah": that is, out of the intentional and the unintentional, the beautiful and the ugly, something emerges. The good deeds remain, and the faulty elements tend to disappear, allowing other aspects to come to the fore. Even where something is primarily evil, no particle or spark of goodness is lost. The sparks, connecting, finally manifest themselves, sometimes after many generations, and in a striking way. It is like a recessive gene that may pass from one generation to the next without any sign of its existence, until with the passage of time and genetic recombining, it is revealed as inherent strength. If ultimately, a pure and rare quality emerges in one descendant, then that bestows meaning to the existence of the whole long line of generations that carried the kernel of the quality within it. So it was with Lot, who had some superior attributes that were not destroyed. Lot in Sodom placed himself in great danger for the sake of hospitality. And his daughters, despite the vileness of their deed, acted as much from the wish to preserve the human species—as it seemed to them—as from passion or lust. It is even possible to detect a veiled similarity between the act of Lot's daughters and Ruth's approach to Boaz many generations later. There was a deep commitment to the continuation of the line, the need to hold fast to the thread of generations, both in the delicacy of Ruth's hint and in the crudeness of Lot's daughters' act. Yet it is the good intention that persisted through time.

Ruth was the daughter of Eglon, King of Moab, a descendant of the line of Balak, who, according to the sages, evinced reverence for the God of Israel and for prophecy. Eglon, too, rose in honor of the one who brought him God's word. The assumption is that noble characteristics and qualities—"holy sparks"—never disappear or are altogether lost but are merely hidden from sight. Like subterranean water, they eventually burst forth to the surface, having undergone generations of purification to cleanse them of their initial impurities and pollution.

The aspect of finding oneself liberated from all external bondage to the past and of emerging unhesitant and without inhibition is very evident in Ruth. It is forcefully revealed in her conversation with Naomi, her dead husband's mother, when Naomi told her two daughters-in-law to leave. Naomi's stand here was clear and practical, even from a halachic point of view: these daughters-in-law were no longer bound to her legally or financially, and nothing remained but for them to return where they belonged. Orpah, the other daughter-in-law, did return to her home and became once more part of the gentile world. (The sages trace the origins of Goliath and his brothers back to Orpah, as the antithesis of David, who was one of Ruth's descendants. Orpah represents the Gentiles' contact with Israel—a contact that became increasingly estranged, until the final confrontation, which the sages call "the defeat of the sons of the kissed one by the sons of the cleaven one.")

What is surprising in Ruth is not only her cleaving to her mother-in-law but the fact that she joined her whole inner life to Naomi's: a woman of another nation, with different beliefs and customs. Furthermore, it was a life that held no promise for the foreseeable future. Nonetheless, Ruth persisted in accompanying Naomi to the end; and although the end was, in a sense, happy, not only for Ruth personally but also for the magnificent chain of generations that followed, this end was not apparent at the beginning. The act that began the chain was free and willing and did not anticipate any recompense.

To be sure, in the years prior to her husband's death, Ruth had certainly moved closer to the Jewish People. It was inconceivable in those days (and for many subsequent generations), that a woman would not adopt her husband's religion, customs, and values. Both Ruth and Orpah, in joining a Jewish family, underwent this change. However, the Jewish family in question was, to some extent, cut off from its roots. This was a family that had found it appropriate and fitting to leave Bethlehem and move to another country, which—albeit not totally strange and hostile—was not Jewish. This was no mere departure from the Land in a physical sense but meant leaving also its values and its Jewish way of life. The meaning of such emigration is strikingly revealed in the words of David—a child of Ruth's son—when he was forced to flee from *Eretz Yisrael*: "They have driven me out this day from abiding in the inheritance of the Lord, saying, Go, serve other gods" (1 Samuel 26:19). The assumption was that leaving the Land meant, as the Talmud later expressed it, "refined idolatry."

At the same time, this family of *yordim* or émigrés would have maintained vestiges of their heritage, remnants of Jewish traditions. Their spiritual world, while certainly less perfect and complete than it had been in their homeland, in Judah, was still a world that held great significance for Ruth. It was a world that had for her enough spiritual content to make her go with her mother-in-law to her people, and for Ruth to feel that she had found her place among them even before she knew that she would have a family of her own there. Ruth's statement "thy people shall be my people, and thy God my God" (Ruth 1:16) is not merely an expression of personal harmony with another people but reveals a deep and genuine spiritual connection.

Thus, the bond between Ruth and Naomi was not only personal but deeper and more intimate. For generations, the relationship between a woman and her daughter-in-law had been one of subordination and duty (of the latter to the former), and the prophets speak of the rebellion of a bride against her mother-in-law as an indication of the decline of the times. Even so, any closer connection, much less love, between them was unusual to a degree. In fact, the *Mishnah* lists women who are, in the nature of things, antagonistic to one another, and among them a mother and daughter-in-law. In any case, it is clear that Ruth's feelings toward the land of Judah, its people, and its religion, transcended the ties of family and personal relations. Boaz expressed it when he praised Ruth, saying that she deserved recompense and reward because she had come to shelter under the wings of the Lord (Ruth 2:12): that is, it was evident that Ruth's coming to Bethlehem was a step of fundamental significance. There is no external explanation for her coming;

it was simply done out of a feeling of involvement by a person who had found her proper place among the people of Israel. Above and beyond the chance family connection—canceled out in any case by Elimelech's death, which left Ruth childless—this feeling of belonging caused her to follow Naomi to Bethlehem and her final fulfillment in the house of Boaz. Naomi returned home from Moab; and it seemed that Ruth, too, was coming home, coming to seek refuge under the protection of the Almighty.

To some extent, the relationship of Ruth and Boaz stands on the fact that he saw in her, from their very first meeting, things that other people did not see. For others, Ruth was first and foremost a foreigner and, as such, an object of suspicion, if not of hatred. It was better to keep a distance from her as a foreigner, because she was only a poor convert in an alien land, without family and without protection. In stating that he did not wish to mar his own inheritance, the kinsman who was called upon to enter some kind of levirate marriage with Ruth meant that he did not want to marry a woman who was defective, in the sense that she was a convert, a Moabitess, a foreigner, or to "contaminate" himself with something so doubtful. This suspicion and hostility were very real. However, according to the sages, Boaz was one of the respected men of Bethlehem, a judge of the tribe of Judah; and he saw things in a different way. Beyond the fact that she was a poor, foreign convert, he saw Ruth's inner being, and this is what he cared about. To Boaz, Ruth had come to seek protection under the wings of the *Shekhinah*; and even before he could consider any personal relationship with her, he tried to encourage her, to support her, and to bring her closer to his world.

Boaz and the kinsman express two different attitudes to proselytes: on the one hand, a fear of the alien and unknown, a skepticism in regard to the motives of the convert, a natural suspicion of those who have crossed over by those who have never deviated from their own framework. On the other hand, there is a deep feeling of attraction and sympathy for the convert. In the Midrash, it is expressed in a parable: A shepherd has a large flock of sheep. A deer enters the fold. The shepherd tells his herdsmen to treat the deer with special care. The herdsmen ask why, with such a large flock, the shepherd should concern himself with this one deer. The shepherd tells them, "My sheep have only this fold, while this deer has the whole world to choose from. Yet he chose my flock, and it is therefore fitting that I should give him special care."

This attitude sums up many *mitzvot* that require us to favor the proselyte in our midst, someone who has the choice of belonging elsewhere and who, nevertheless, chooses to enter the Jewish framework. The convert deserves special consideration and a special relationship. The Book of Ruth is a beautiful portrayal of a true proselyte, unique in the Scriptures in that she is described as being wholly pure.

The description of Ruth's "homecoming" to her real, inner being is a spiritual odyssey: we see her shed the trappings of her former existence, the connection with her family and origins. We see her undeterred by the difficulties of her new life, her fidelity to her commitment even when she is faced with the indifference of the local people; and finally, we see all these pale into insignificance in relation to Ruth's inner soul. We see that same ancient kernel of sanctity, that same spark that had burned unseen for generations, find its rightful place within the people of Israel.

15

Samuel

THE RELIGIOUS RENAISSANCE

amuel is one of the great prophets, the guiding spirit of an age that marked a major transition in the history of the Jewish people.

A measure of his stature and historical significance is the fact that two books of the Bible bear his name, even though only the first part of 1 Samuel deals directly with the prophet. The rest of this book mainly describes the relationship between Saul and David, while 2 Samuel is devoted to David's mature years. Moreover, in Psalm 99:6, we find "Moses and Aaron among his priests, and Samuel among them that call upon his name"—a statement that has led the sages to conclude that Samuel was equal in eminence to Moses and Aaron.

---

1 Samuel 1-16 and 28:3-25.

Elsewhere in the Bible, we are given only subtle hints about Samuel's greatness. In a few fascinating, very human passages, we learn about the circumstances of his birth; about his father, Elkanah, and his mother, Hannah; about Eli, the priest, and the boy Samuel who heard the voice of God. Yet all this does not offer much enlightenment about the nature of the adult Samuel who became a prophet and leader of stature, even while we are drawn to the figure of the little boy in the mantle his mother made for him. Incidentally, it is of that same garment that became so much a part of him that a *midrash* says that it grew as he grew and was with him till he died; it was the same garment in which he appeared to Saul when the Witch of En-dor was made to call up Samuel's spirit from the dead: "An old man . . . covered with a mantle" (1 Samuel 28:14).

To ascertain the true power and significance of Samuel's personality, we have to read between the lines of the biblical text and see him in his historical perspective.

Samuel ended one period in the history of the nation and brought about, not necessarily of his own volition, a new age. He was the last of the Judges, and he initiated the reign of the kings of Israel, anointing the first monarch, Saul. Samuel, therefore, was the link between the disunity and lack of social order that characterized the time of the Judges, and the more structured state that was introduced when he put Saul, and later David, on the throne. Samuel was the driving force behind the welding of the tribes into an organized political entity, transferring authority as he did from the Judges to the first kings. Albeit, as we read (1 Samuel 8), he did this reluctantly and under divine duress. At the same time, this historic role does not reflect the whole of Samuel's personality. He was not a mere tool, charged with a specific task; but he himself made a religious contribution of vast historical importance. Indeed, later sages see in him much more than the one who inaugurated the house of David.

In order better to understand Samuel's profound effect on Jewish history, it might be useful to reconstruct the social and political conditions of his times. According to the Book of Judges, one of the decisive factors behind the general political instability of that period was the oft-mentioned fact that "in those days there was no king in Israel" (Judges 18:1, 19:1, 21:25). That is to say, there was no stable civic structure beyond a loose national consensus, which operated only under exceptional circumstances, such as a war against a common invader or the need to bring order to one or another of the tribes. During the rule of the Judges, therefore, the sociopolitical foundation of the nation was unreliable, prey to outside pressures, and dependent upon the emergence of a leader who, at any given time, could rally all the tribes around the banner of a common cause. In other words, there was no central authority to establish and maintain a framework of law and order. With the establishment of the kingdom, all this changed; and although other problems followed in the wake of the new social and political order, it did bring stability into both civic and religious life.

The time of the Judges has been described in terms of wavelike movements of advance and regression: the people abandon the Lord, the people return to the Lord; a period of crisis is followed by a period of restoration. The Judges were not only military and civil leaders but also, to some degree, men of faith. Their influence resided not only in their unique personalities, in their military genius, but also in their role as spiritual messengers. Almost all the Judges appeared in the name of God or, at least, claimed to act in His name. Practically every one of the Judges made some declaration to this effect, from Ehud who came to speak the word of the Lord (Judges 3:15-31), to Gideon with his cry: "The sword of the Lord, and of Gideon" (Judges 7:18).

Nonetheless, it seems that, for the duration of the rule of the Judges—a period that lasted a few hundred years—there was a decline in, and degeneration of, religious values. After the early generations of Joshua and the elders, the Children of Israel settled down in the Promised Land and began to pursue worldly success and personal gain. As noted in the *Midrash Tanna Devei Eliyahu*, at that time all of Israel, from the simple folk to the learned elders, sat each in his own vineyard and sought only to sink roots firmly into the soil of the Land. Just as a much later generation of settlers said of themselves that they came not only to build the Land but to be built by it, so life then revolved around the cultivation of the soil. It was a physical, earth-bound life, and spiritual values had no place in it. Idolatrous practices, such as those described in the Book of Judges and substantiated by numerous archeological discoveries throughout the country, were common. The worship of God was not abandoned, however, nor was it replaced by a cult of other gods. Rather, there was a spiritual decline, a dilution and dulling of religious feeling.

The sanctuary at Shiloh continued to function after a fashion, and the faithful continued to come there and to support the priests, even if without much enthusiasm. The Levite youth described in Judges 17 who went round seeking to make a living as a "religious guide" was a child of his times, a symptom of the general religious decline. The lad would have preferred to be at the sanctuary at Shiloh; but, when he was unable to support himself there, he was ready to compromise his essential religious role. He was even prepared to serve as a household priest to the graven images in Micha's house. This attitude in itself was characteristic of the spirit of the times: the graven image, the statue, was seen not as idolatrous but merely as another variation on the theme of the ritual. It was a fashion that marked another stage in the spiritual degeneration of a period dominated by a peasant class, by farmers, bound and limited by the daily round of work, family, seasons. Many expressions of this type of worship were cultist and local; images were usually of Ashtoret or one of the domestic deities and were more in the nature of amulets or totems than devotional objects. The fact is that the Jew of this period still felt himself to be a thinking person, who proudly worshiped the one true God. Nevertheless, he reckoned that it could do no harm to have a little image around to take care of matters of prosperity and fertility. The period of the Judges cannot be considered as totally lacking in spiritual understanding, military unity, or political stability, but all these elements were clearly affected by the widespread religious decline and by the sad fact that fundamental belief was reduced to mere superstition. We read in 1 Samuel that "the word of the Lord was precious in those days; there was no open vision" (3:1): that is, there were no prophets or visionaries in Israel; and hence, there was no spiritual insight.

When Samuel walked onto the stage of history, a new element entered with him. This element, even if not completely innovative, was a renewal of original revelation and had profound implications for the future, ushering in, as it did, a new social order as well: the age of the First Temple and the kingdom.

This is not to say that Samuel was the originator of the idea of the kingdom. On the contrary, he fought against it with all his might. Nevertheless, it was paradoxically he who made it possible by restoring the national and religious ideals of the Jewish people. It was his insistence on a unified expression of these ideals that defined the goals and aspirations of a monarchy and even made it a logical necessity. Such an idea would have been simply inconceivable two hundred, or even one hundred, years earlier.

The greatness of Samuel's contribution is best seen against the background of the sanctuary at Shiloh, where the sons of Eli served. Eli himself was a decent old man, perhaps even something of a saint, who, if not a great spiritual leader, devotedly carried out his priestly tasks. His sons, too, were probably courageous and loyal, as evidenced in their last hour when, faithful to their role as priests and bearers of the Ark of the Covenant, they accompanied it to war and were killed at its side. Nevertheless, the spiritual atmosphere of the sanctuary at Shiloh was one of sleepiness, sloth, gluttony, and, above all, a vast indifference. One receives the impression from the biblical text that the sanctuary and its ritual were part of an old tradition—of little interest to anyone, not even to the priests themselves. They were simply in attendance and made sure that they received their allotted share of the sacrifice—a very pragmatic aspect of the ritual—and, on the whole, appeared to have paid scant attention to the underlying religious meaning of the rites. Altogether, the ceremony seems to have lacked religious significance or depth. Against this background, Samuel appeared as a new force, an entirely unprecedented phenomenon. Not only was he a prophet, but his very origins were linked to the sanctuary, as is revealed in the story of his mother, Hannah.

Before Samuel's birth, Hannah had come to the sanctuary not only to perform the regular ritual purification ceremony for women but to pour out her heart before God. This direct prayer must have been surprising even to Eli, the high priest, since spontaneous, passionate worship was unusual in those days. Hannah is shown as a woman of profound religious feeling capable of uniting her soul in prayer. Samuel's father, Elkanah, is mentioned in later commentaries with considerable respect as a pious man in an impious generation. It was in this spirit that Samuel was raised.

He had been pledged to the sanctuary, to become a man of God from childhood, even before his birth: "There shall no razor come upon his head" (1 Samuel 1:11). But in contrast to Samson, that other consecrated man of the age, Samuel's whole life was one of selfless devotion to the ritual and divine service of the Lord. He came from outside the ranks of the hereditary priesthood, which earned its livelihood by performing the rites and ceremonies; yet he became the first to assume that task with the profound dedication it demanded. To Samuel, the sanctuary, the ritual and worship, were not old customs, universally accepted even if in disrepute, but a source of inspiration and enlightenment. His task went beyond that of the priest to that of the prophet; he was a man with a vision—a vision that consisted of a renewal of the ancient faith. Samuel said things that were not new, but he said them with new emphasis; and elements of his prophecy have become part of Jewish religious consciousness.

He revived the idea, which became a point of departure for later prophets, that the ritual was not a substitute for the spiritual aspects of religion. He was outraged by its denigration into empty ceremony and by the neglect of the discipline of living according to divine commandment. In short, Samuel returned to the basic elements of Jewish faith: a way of life that was total and obligatory. After generations of decline, in which the people were sunk in ignorance and spiritual sloth, Samuel was the first seriously to relate to his own spiritual world—and he did so when he was still very young and despite his lack of hereditary authority.

Samuel's innovations, like those of many religious revolutionaries, were masked as a return to the significant elements of the ancient faith. More than most men who are aware of a social need and take on the challenge of meeting it, Samuel was wholly and wholeheartedly involved in his mission—hence, the saying that Samuel is akin to both Moses and Aaron. Just as the Children of Israel were slaves in Egypt, so, too, was Israel at the time of the Judges a slave people bound to the earth, with no clear vision of heaven. It was Samuel who initiated the religious renaissance of his generation, thus filling the role of both Moses and Aaron. He did not need to say anything new; he simply related to the known elements of the religion as though they were new, and established the social and cultural framework that made possible the development of the kingdom of David.

16

Saul

THE DANGEROUS INNOCENCE

aul, the first king of the Jewish people, was, in his life as in his death, a tragic figure.

Prior to Saul, there had been some weak attempts to assume kingship—as, for instance, by Abimelech, son of Gideon, some generations earlier. However, there was neither divine nor temporal legitimacy to Abimelech's appointment, and he was not very different from other tyrants of the times who seized power in the absence of genuine opposition. Saul, however, was not only king, the ruler, but also the Chosen One of Israel, the "Lord's Anointed." This is extremely important because it formed the essential perspective from which Saul saw himself and the world around him and determined the attitude of others toward him. Even after having lost confidence in

1 Samuel 9—2 Samuel 1.

Saul's powers to rule the kingdom and when flee-
ing from his mad and pointless pursuit, David was
still unable to divest himself of his respect and
veneration for the anointed of God. This is an
aspect of kingship seldom encountered in the
history of other rulers.

The critical point in Saul's life had been his
meeting with, and subsequent anointing by, the
prophet Samuel. The suddenness, the unexpect-
edness of this meeting had a significance for Saul
that went far beyond the ceremonial act of pour-
ing oil over his head. The ritual was intended to
open a new dimension of being in Saul, followed
as it was by his joining with the band of prophets
and, like them, seeing visions and uttering prophecies. Saul's visions were more than a passing
phenomenon. Significantly, he seems to have retained this power, although he never actually
became a prophet, as we are informed in 1 Samuel
19:23. Indeed, it became a sort of saying—"Is Saul
also among the prophets?" (1 Samuel 10:11)—
because he prophesied in rather strange fashion.

Be that as it may, it is clear that Saul's prophetic
powers resulted from his anointing; and if one per-
mits oneself to speculate a little, it may be possible
to see, in the inner transformation of this tall,
healthy youth, the beginnings of a psychological
development that eventually led to his decline.

The sages have depicted Saul as a combination
of extreme shyness and great courage. One of the

midrash commentaries hints that Saul belonged to those of the tribe of Benjamin who were supposed to lie in wait and catch a wife from among the daughters of Shiloh, sent to dance in the vineyards (Judges 21:19-23). According to this commentary, Saul was too bashful to catch one of the maidens, and she had to run after him. This may be part of the background to that oddly phrased, derisive rebuke by Saul of his son Jonathan: "Thou son of the perverse rebellious woman" (I Samuel 20:30)—that is, son of the woman who had dared to pursue him.

In the *Midrash*, we find the description of Saul as he first appears: a heroic youth, tall and slender, confused, but normal and healthy in every way. It is the meeting with Samuel that creates the deep fissure in his soul and that, together with the prophetic experience that follows it, seems to have dramatically unsettled him. From this point on, he was transformed; he was no longer an ordinary private person—Saul, son of Kish—but the Anointed of the Lord, with all the attendant expansion of his faculties, making him a vessel of wisdom and courage. His sensitivity and vulnerability also increased. The slightest touch became an injury to his pride, and he was visited by an evil spirit (described as coming from God) that weakened and ultimately destroyed him.

A fascinating parallel to the story of Saul is that of his son Jonathan. In many ways, Jonathan was

Saul's double, revealing his wholly sympathetic and likable aspect. Jonathan was what Saul might have been had the latter not had to undergo the trauma of kingship, of being taken so suddenly from his flocks to be made King of Israel, the Chosen of the Lord.

Saul's whole life—indeed, his very personality—is tragic. Much has been written in the attempt to probe his soul, to describe his inner struggles and his baleful influence on the people closest to him. Are we, in fact, confronted here with a single personality? Is there one factor common to the whole of this complex and divided life? Or do we have here a split personality: on the one hand, strong and sane, the good king who did his utmost for the welfare of the nation; and, on the other, the man obsessed by fears and doubts who pursued the people around him with imaginings so wild they were little short of madness?

The Bible tends to view its heroes and, indeed, all men as fallible. They are not artificial constructs of definable parts or ideal oneness; they are almost always shown from different angles. Even the most beloved biblical heroes have their faults as well as their virtues. David, one of the outstanding figures in Jewish history, is revealed not only in his greatness and splendor but also in his weakness, even in his sin.

How, then, are we to view the story of Saul's decline and fall? Does it indicate an inner sickness, or is it just one of those terribly truthful descriptions of a hero? Was Saul a pitiful creature tormented by uncontrollable fits of paranoia, or was there a profound inner order and logic to his life? To answer the question, let us look at a certain aspect of Saul's personality that may prove to be the key to much else in the biblical story. It is that aspect that reveals both what was finest in the man and what caused him to make his worst mistakes. Saul was a man who allowed his heart to control his head. Feeling and sentiment governed all his thoughts and actions, and he was unable to digress from their prescribed course. Subjectively speaking, these sentiments were genuine, but they did not permit him to act rationally. That was Saul's dominating characteristic, especially when we compare him with David. In everything that David did, from the greatest to the smallest of his actions, he seemed to present an element of sobriety, of clear-headedness. Even when he got himself entangled in sin or folly, that element of lucidity, the power to control his feelings, was never quite lost. One may compare David's superficial attack of madness with Saul's obsessiveness and note the contrast between Saul's fits, which left him helpless, and David's calculated play acting.

This characteristic of impulsive emotionalism and the absence of adequate thought or planning was the expression of Saul's personality and dictated the form of his life. In its positive aspect, it gave his life a certain tone, a certain nobility, a genuine sincerity. Saul remained a person who was spared any doubts concerning his innermost feelings and who retained, until the last, a vast amount of enviable innocence and simplicity.

In contrast to many other neurotic people, Saul's major personality trait was not complex or knotty, although it caused intricate problems. Saul was simply extreme in allowing his feelings to dominate his reason. In this, he showed unusual unity and wholeness that caused the sages to declare that he was unblemished by wickedness or deviousness. They maintained that this was precisely the reason the kingship did not stem from Saul: without participating in the faults of men, a man cannot rule. David, for instance, was a man of many faults, but these did not bring about his downfall.

Coming as Saul did from an ancient line of a small, long-suffering tribe that had preserved for itself a special place in Israel, he personified the best of the rural aristocracy. With his forthright manner, his loyalty and simplicity, he was the honest, simple man brought from behind the plow to become king.

With penetrating psychological insight, the sages have noted, concerning Saul's straightforward character, that he who is merciful to the cruel will end up by being cruel to the merciful. At first glance, this may seem to be a contradictory pronouncement. The point is that, although these qualities of cruelty and mercifulness are contradictory, they do express an element of Saul's psyche: the inability to maintain equilibrium within any framework. Such a one is always a captive of his own impulses and is carried along by them from one extreme to the other. Hence, this King Saul who could not bring himself to kill the Amalekites—even though, under divine command, he had gone to war to do so—was the same man who could give the order to kill all the people of the city of priests: men, women, and children. The same person who was merciful to the worst of his enemies was also extravagantly cruel toward completely innocent people. In Saul, these tendencies of compassion and cruelty were not always contradictory. Both expressed his inability to control his feelings, whether of revenge against the priests, or compassion for the enemy, or hostility to David.

When we examine the whole personality of Saul, without lingering on its emotional aspects, what we have is not a shifty, unstable soul but a man who simply never achieved the maturity to realize that one cannot always depend upon the heart. Therefore, in all of Saul's sins—those of mercy and those of cruelty, those of indecision and those of impulse—we find that element that gives them the dimension of tragedy: in almost everything he did, even in his worst deeds, Saul was unfalteringly, naïvely committed to what he believed to be the right course of action.

There is the impression in the biblical story that Saul was not always aware when he was sinning, but acted always under the illusion that what he was doing was right. Even when pursuing David, he was convinced that he was doing so in the interests of the kingdom, and not out of personal resentment. Saul still loved David, even when he tried to kill him—as one must realize in order to understand the complexity of their relationship. Saul was obsessed by the belief that his kingdom was threatened; and he felt that, at all costs, he had to transfer the legacy of kingship in orderly fashion. Although he saw David as a danger to this orderly transfer, his love for him was not affected, and in calling him "my son," Saul spoke impulsively and without duplicity.

Saul's strange relationship with David reflects the chief difference in their personalities. David's attitude to Saul was made up of an undisguised fear for his own life and a sense of profound awe for the "anointed of God." David was the personification of mind in control of heart. This sense of thoughtful reckoning and duty was always far ahead of his own personal inclinations. This kind of personality is obviously preferable when it comes to running a country.

On the fall of Saul's kingdom the sages have commented that indeed Saul had no blemish; his sins were not sins of degradation, of lust for women, or even of personal hatred—the vices of the kings of Judah. At the same time, this very purity made it impossible for him to govern. To direct the destiny of a nation requires a man who knows his own failings and has intimate knowledge of the failings of humankind. He must be a man who can withstand insult and injury, and who has a keen grasp of political actualities—always the product of specific times, men, and circumstances. These qualities are what David possessed almost to perfection, while Saul, with his simple forthright personality, his naïve sense of being the anointed of God and therefore in touch with higher worlds, was caught in a web of events that defeated him. In a sense, his failure is the failure of the better man, the failure of one chosen for a task that did not need a better man, only a wiser and more capable one.

Saul's simplicity of soul, his inability to vanquish his own heart and feelings for the sake of diplomacy and political reality, his very spontaneity of expression, whether of pity or of anger, are all part of a distinctive personality, one both noble and gracious. In the end, it was these very traits that destroyed Saul and brought to the throne of Israel the man more suited to the task.

17

Michal

THE PRINCESS AND
THE SHEPHERD

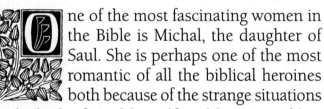ne of the most fascinating women in the Bible is Michal, the daughter of Saul. She is perhaps one of the most romantic of all the biblical heroines both because of the strange situations in which she found herself and because of her tragic fate.

At the same time, the biblical text shows us a Michal who was almost totally passive, who spoke and acted very little for herself. Our glimpses of her are fragmentary, as though we were peeping at her through cracks in the shutters, through the rents and tears in the fabric of family life, into the inner palace and her private life there.

1 Samuel 18:18-27 and 19:11-17: 2 Samuel 3:14-16 and 6:20-23.

The few words Michal utters are important in providing an understanding of her character. The power of the biblical account lies in a few short, sharp lines, sketches of the people and events in question. On the whole, we are told almost nothing of the thoughts of the heroes; there are no complex and complicated dialogues, no character "buildup." From this point of view, biblical narrative is in marked contrast to Greek drama. The latter, in almost all its forms, rests largely on monologues in which the heroes explain their experiences and feelings. When the monologue does not suffice, the chorus fills in the gaps in the story and carries the narrative forward. Thus, the author has the opportunity to express his own educational, moral, and philosophical ideas. In the Bible, we find almost none of these devices. Yet the narrative is often strikingly clear and provides us with true-to-life multidimensional figures. Thus, we discover Michal in three different situations, each one of which shows us a different aspect. The combination of the three pictures, the three situations, enables us to reconstruct not only the events that characterize each one, but also to understand her personality.

Michal is first introduced with the words: "And Michal, Saul's daughter, loved David" (1 Samuel 18:20), hinting at a story of first love. We next meet her when, after David's escape from Saul, she is given to another man, Palti ben Laish (1 Samuel

25:44); and in the third story, we witness a short conversation, a very unpleasant scene, between David and Michal (2 Samuel 6:20-23), in which she comments on the way he dances. Taken in isolation, none of these brief passages presents a full picture; but together, they give us a general portrait of relationships, a portrait that illuminates and reveals aspects of David's character as much as it does those of Michal.

One point that is perhaps crucial to Michal's personality, and for understanding the relationship between her and David, is actually linked to the relationship between the tribes of Judah and Benjamin. Saul and Michal were truly representative of the image and essence of their whole tribe, Benjamin, with all its power and advantages and its concomitant weaknesses. The most marked facet of Michal's character is that she was an aristocrat, a princess. She was the daughter of the nobility, not only because her father was king, but because her whole family was noble. It was a nobility that had beauty and elegance, along with weaknesses. Such aristocratic figures may often include something anemic, a certain inability to adapt to awkward situations. We often find in them passivity instead of action, silence where there should be speech, and thoughtless chatter where there should be silence.

David's is an entirely different personality. As can be seen from his words and his Psalms, David sees himself as a shepherd, a small-town boy. To be sure, he grew and prospered, he became a national hero, but there remained in him something of the simple youth from the small town. David belongs to the tribe of Judah, a tribe of shepherds connected to the desert and, to some extent, the nomadic life. He personally experienced the hardship of the wilderness and desert. His off-handed boast that "Also the lion and the bear has thy servant smitten" (1 Samuel 17:36) describes encounters typical of life at the edge of the desert. Later, in engaging in the collection of what could be called "protection money," David is merely exhibiting the other side of the same shepherd-boy personality. To a certain extent, David represents earthiness both in its rootedness, its deep connection to things, and in its touch of vulgarity.

The tension between the aristocrat and the shepherd, an attraction and repulsion, is evidenced in the three confrontations between Michal and David. In their first encounter David appears as the victorious hero, promised the hand of a princess. We can picture Michal, the young girl reared as a king's daughter in a very closed environment, even more so than was common for unmarried maidens. She lived in the shy, restrained, and reserved atmosphere of the house of Saul.

In contrast to these reserved people—some of whom, like Jonathan, were heroic and beautiful in body and soul—someone like David appeared. He was simpler, more earthy, undoubtedly of handsome appearance, and a hero of war. Very understandably, an attachment was formed, a first love, involving the closeted young girl from the aristocratic family. Michal fell in love with the village hero; and his simplicity—or crudeness—was not disturbing to her but doubtless had a certain charm of its own. The same characteristics have had a singular magic for many other young maidens, in similar circumstances, throughout history. Out of this attraction was born a great love: Michal, the daughter of Saul, loved David. A special relationship was created between them, and even Michal, never overtalkative, showed it, so that Saul, for all his introversion, sensed what was going on. From this first contact, Michal and David were bound by a tie of love that remained constant, despite all the problems that followed. It remained steadfast in the face of the pressures later created by Saul and was unshaken by the triangle of relations between Saul, David, and Jonathan.

Michal did not often act of her own accord; yet until her last moments with David, she remained loyal, and even more than loyal, to him. In fact, she was even prepared to betray her father for David's sake, as when she tricked Saul by smuggling David out of the house to enable him to escape Saul's ire. The situation is reminiscent—and not only from the point of view of "plot"—of the relationship between Rachel and Laban, perhaps not surprisingly, since Michal, of the tribe of Benjamin, was a direct descendant of Rachel. The story of David's escape (1 Samuel 19:13) contains a key word identical to one in the story of Laban's pursuit of Jacob and the theft of his household images (Genesis 31:34). These two instances are the only references in the Bible to household or family idols. In both cases, they are treated as a means of cheating the father. In both cases, the inner motive is similar: the bond with the man, with the new hero, is so deep that it apparently erases all other ties. This special bond between David and Michal remains to the end.

In the next passage, the weakness of the aristocracy is disclosed. While in the first situation, we find a mutual attraction, the combination and pairing of beauty and heroism, of the old nobility and the "man of the people," in the second, we find Michal's surrender and passivity when given to another man. She was given away to Palti ben Laish, a man who was possibly a friend of the family, of the house of Saul. She moved with him across the Jordan, where she remained with him for several years. The Talmud tells us several things about Palti ben Laish, who was apparently closer to Saul's house than to David's, and about his attitude to Michal. However, if we look at Michal herself, we are given a glimpse of her essential being, by what she did not do. When Palti was forced to renounce Michal, it is said that he went "along with her weeping behind her" (2 Samuel 3:16). But Michal did not cry. In a way, it seems as if she had lost her active personality in this great crisis, acting no longer as a human being but as an object, a chattel. She was taken and returned by Palti ben Laish—in silence.

We can imagine Michal's emotional crisis in different ways, but a crisis it surely was. Her heart was broken. She had been handed over to another man whom she did not love, and the impression is somehow created that she was no longer capable of caring for anyone, not even for David. The parting from him (which she believed to be final) and her being handed over to Palti ben Laish broke her spirit until she reached a point of total detachment. This emotional detachment was partly an expression of her aristocratic nature. The nobility was superior; they did not make scenes or have stormy fights, nor did they destroy social structures. Michal did not rebel; she did not try to escape from the entanglement by some extreme means, such as suicide, as did her father Saul at the end of his days. She could protest her lot, but instead she broke, and what remained was the outer shell of a personality from which the heart was missing. From this point onward, Michal responded to everything that happened with total passivity, the passivity of one who is past caring.

She continued to function, to fulfill her role in accordance with her status, and she did this right to the end of her life. But inwardly something had snapped; her personality was no longer what it was, and she was concerned only with the externals of behavior.

The Michal of the first meeting with David was not the same woman who was returned to him several years later. She had undergone not so much a personality change as a kind of death. The heart, the emotion, the excitement had gone out of the woman, and what remained was the shell: an aristocrat, and nothing more.

All this is sharply expressed in the final episode of the Michal–David relationship, which reveals a clash between two cultures as well as between two totally different individuals. It was a clash between David, so very earthy, passionate, and enthusiastic, and Michal, reserved, introverted, and deeply concerned with propriety. Michal's rebuke to David is a key to her whole personality. She neither saw nor related to the spiritual significance of bringing the Ark of the Covenant to Jerusalem. She knew that it was an important celebration, and what bothered her on this great occasion was the fact that David had exposed himself when dancing in front of the maidservants. How could he do such a thing! The sages have already pointed out the marvelous sense of modesty in Saul's family: the way in which he went deep, deep into the cave when he wished to "cover his feet." That same horror of nakedness, which is characteristic of all Semitic cultures, was marked in Saul, in his personal relations as in his public behavior. He had a fear of exposing himself. Hence the covering up, the layers upon layers of garments and clothing.

In contrast to this modesty and circumspection, so characteristic of the aristocracy and nobility everywhere, at all periods of history, we find David. David did not stop to consider how he was dancing, how he was behaving, how he appeared to others. For Michal, the fact of exposure was less important than the humiliation—as she saw it—of cheapening himself before the masses, of descending to their level. She was injured by the fact that David did not treat his throne with respect, that he had no sense of the majesty of kingship, of being divinely chosen to lead. She was the daughter of the nobility contrasted with the man she actually regarded as common, as a boor, as one who may have taken up the reigns of government but not the grandeur of the kingship.

David, for his part, was no less sharp in his response to Michal, and his sharpness is illuminating. He juxtaposed these contrasting elements, comparing his election as king not necessarily with Michal but with what she represented: the house of Saul, her father. David claimed that the choice of the Almighty had fallen rather on someone like him: a man who expressed genuine feelings, real emotions, the quality of passion, the ability to experience misfortune without breaking, the ability to withstand hardship, and still to rejoice, to express his joy and reveal himself.

The sages' saying that the kingship of the house of Saul did not continue because he had no fault, finds an echo in the relations between David and Michal. Outwardly, she was flawless, cold, and noble, the ideal woman viewed from afar. David, in contrast, was passionate, fiery in everything he did, in his virtues and in his sins; he had his flaws and his failings, and he also had the strength to rise above them.

In this clash of opposing life views, the two personalities are revealed, each in its own light. Michal's plight arises not only from her reserve and inhibition but from the tragedy of this aristocratic woman's love for a man so very different.

Michal's heart was broken because David could never be wholly hers: he could never fit her notions of the perfect, and she could not accept him as he was. She could be happy neither with him nor without him.

18

Solomon

THE WISDOM
AND ITS LIMITS

King Solomon is an unusual example of a son who is not overshadowed by his remarkable father.

It is true that, for all his greatness, Solomon created the circumstances that brought about the division of David's kingdom and the diminution of its splendor. Various actions that Solomon took, including excessive taxation and the dismantling of the strong military force, certainly contributed to the collapse of the centralistic regime after his death. Yet, we do not have here just another instance of an empire founded by a father and left in ruins by his son.

Solomon is a great man in his own right, from every vantage point an outstanding personality. With all their differences, David and Solomon

1 Kings 1-11.

were both unforgettable personalities. Just as there was a special magic about David, there was a singular enchantment to Solomon's reign as well. Not without justification are the reigns of David and Solomon sometimes viewed as a single entity, a unified historic whole. Both reigns evoke echoes of magnificence and grandeur, albeit each of a different style.

Temperamentally, David and Solomon seem to have been almost complete opposites: David was an adventurous spirit, and much of his life was spent in wandering and in battle. He was a man of war who knew how to contend with difficult men and situations. Solomon, on the other hand, is not a fighter; he does not engage in bloody battle. His is ostensibly a tranquil life marked by stability and creativity.

The apparent chasm between the two personalities is, to a great extent, imaginary. There are many aspects of Solomon's personality that can be traced to David. Furthermore, Solomon not only fulfills David's final wishes (the grand plans as well as the personal requests); he also perpetuates, in his own style, David's line of thought.

The prophet Nathan relates Solomon's name, *Shlomo*, to the fact that he is a man of peace (*shalom*); however, it was not moral objections that kept Solomon from spilling blood. He merely had more effective means of accomplishing the same goals. Solomon, through complex means, was able to achieve things that David sought through violence, and many of these accomplishments became permanent features. Solomon may therefore be said to have been the fulfillment of David's hopes, the son who ultimately reflects the innermost qualities of the father.

David conceivably would have preferred one of his other sons as his successor, a son like Amnon or Absalom, who perhaps outwardly resembled him more. They were more handsome, more striking, and more dynamic than Solomon. Absalom, for one, certainly does personify the undeniable charisma that was David's, that ability to arouse love from almost all those around him. But these sons' actions revealed that they had only absorbed the external charm of their father's personality, not its essence.

Beyond David's endearing charm there lay another quality: an ability to pursue certain objectives with consistency and steely purposefulness, at the complete sacrifice of his personal emotions. There were a few things that were for him vital, and for which he was prepared to forfeit much that was dear to him. One was the struggle for a united kingdom under strong central rule. Another—his very essence—was his worship of the Lord. This quality of David's is lacking in those other sons who aspired to kingship, but it is striking in Solomon. Not only does David's dynasty continue through Solomon, so does his personality, although in a more sophisticated and subtle way.

If there is one trait for which Solomon is renowned, it is his wisdom. It is first mentioned in the Bible by David himself when he told his son, who was then only sixteen—or even younger—on the latter's ascent to the throne: "Thou art a wise man" (1 Kings 2:9). All of Solomon's deeds and accomplishments were a conscious expression of this wisdom, which was both profound and sensible. It was never a restricted sagacity, confined to any one aspect of learning or of life, but extended over the widest possible range of the practical and the possible. Not only was Solomon wise, but he could transmit his wisdom to others and, like his father, could enchant his hearers to a remarkable degree. Visitors—among them, the Queen of Sheba—came to him from many countries to hear his illuminating pronouncements and to look upon his greatness.

The wide range of Solomon's wisdom can be seen in his political strategems, his courtroom tactics, and in various incidents related in the Bible in an almost offhanded manner. Sometimes it is only between the lines of the Scriptures that his wisdom is evident. For instance, he consciously attempted to dissolve the tribal framework of the people of Israel, establishing a new administrative division of twelve geographical, or geopolitical, provinces that did not clearly corre-

Benaiah was rewarded for his loyalty by being made head of the national army. However, careful examination of later royal appointments will show that the role of commander-in-chief diminished in importance during Solomon's reign. Other official functions became more important and continued to exert real power even after his death. Clearly, these appointments also served to bring about a change in the political balance within the kingdom. Instead of the commander-in-chief being the second most powerful figure after the king, new functions were introduced by Solomon: the scribes who served as foreign ministers, the tax collectors who became responsible for the state treasury, and so forth. He also arranged to have around him a number of private secretaries—royal counselors who played a vital role in creating a new power balance. These functionaries came to play an important part in the administration of the Kingdom of Judah, including "the one who was over the household" (2 Kings 18:18) and became a central figure in later historical developments. The commander-in-chief, on the other hand, remained no more than a military expert in charge of the army, rather than the one who held the kingdom in the palm of his hand, as had Joab in David's time. The commander-in-chief was unable to assert himself or rebel; he became a civil servant, subject to the king's command. This is just another example of Solomon's quiet, efficient way of gaining political ends by social and administrative means.

In the field of foreign affairs, Solomon also introduced remarkable changes. He was the first ruler of Israel who made a significant attempt—to some extent successful—to build up a network of foreign diplomatic and trade relations. David's connection with other countries was based on military alliances of longer or shorter duration. His politics were those of the strong military commander who has broken the balance of power in the Middle East. Solomon, on the other hand, consistently endeavored to build permanent diplomatic relations not only with the great powers of his day but also with less powerful countries. He established a system of political relations that was maintained by all the kings of Judah and of Israel who came after him. It may be pertinent to add that clearly the thousand wives of Solomon were no reflection of an insatiable lust. They were more an expression of the nature of his political associations. His many marriages were for Solomon a means of securing his relations with the great clans and with foreign nations, simply a manifestation of his efforts to gain political ends by means less painful than war. Solomon was perhaps among the first historical personages to live by the slogan "Make love not war."

More than all this, Solomon's famed wisdom not only enabled him to follow the path of peace but also guided him to build the Holy Temple, the great achievement that helped to turn the man into a magnificent myth. It is not for naught that Psalm 72, "Song unto Solomon," has been interpreted as referring both to Solomon and to the Messiah, because both figures represent an age of peace, prosperity, and splendor.

This glorious image of King Solomon is, however, marred by a distressful, sour note, which appears in the biblical account itself. He transgressed several of the negative commandments of the Torah that had to do with kingship: "His wives turned away his heart after other gods" (1 Kings 11:4). Even here, it seems that it was not passion or frivolity that made him susceptible to the demands of his foreign wives. Rather, one may safely assume that Solomon the Wise may have been too clever for his own good. He did not take the worship of alien gods and idolatrous customs seriously but regarded them as nonsense. Solomon's prayer in 1 Kings 8:15-53 is inspiring in its breadth, in its universality, placing the people of Israel and the whole world on the same scale. It is a kind of intellectual treatise attempting to explain the relationship between God the Infinite and the Holy Temple. To a man as wise as Solomon, the pagan cults were almost on a par with the games of children; and because he belittled them thus, he permitted his wives to play their familiar household games, to build little altars, and to perform their inconsequential ceremonies. In this sense, his wives "deflected" his heart—not because he was tempted by them or their cults, but because he underestimated the impact of these cults on others. This was the trap of his cleverness, and he was unable to evaluate the tenacity of minds simpler than his own.

The same may be said of much of his far-sighted diplomacy: he was not perceptive enough to the reactions of the "little man," the people, to his carefully thought-out plans, and he did not notice the hidden flaws that these contained. There was a growing reluctance to pay the heavy taxes, especially with the waning of royal magnificence, and the foreign cults began to undermine the old traditions. It was precisely the simple people who became inflamed and aroused by the idolatrous practices. They could not help but believe that what was good enough for the palace was certainly good enough for them; they required firm guidance and leadership, not confusing examples.

Solomon's great wisdom was his downfall. He could foresee the implications of phenomena hundreds and even thousands of years into the future, but misread the here and now, the common man, the petty temptations. He could not appreciate the effect that his tolerance of religious malpractice was having upon the unlettered multitudes. His great wisdom could not comprehend folly. For all his understanding, he did not suffi-ciently understand fools.

Solomon, the wise man who measured the world by his own standards, who was sure of his ability to increase the number of his wives and keep his heart steady, could not foresee that he would be called a "sinner who causes others to sin," and that his splendid reign was giving birth to many "little conspirators" who would destroy much of what he had built.

19

Elisha

THE PRAGMATIC PROPHET

n both a historical and a religious sense, Elijah and Elisha are a teacher–disciple team, akin to Moses and Joshua. Indeed, Elijah has been more than once likened to Moses, in that both held a forty-day vigil culminating in revelation on Mount Horeb (Sinai), and both had a measure of "other-worldliness" in their makeup and had to leave much of the fulfillment of their revelations to more practical-minded disciples.

Elijah's vision at Mount Horeb, with its fire, windstorm, and the still, small voice, concluded with a mild word of "discharge from active duty." He was told to appoint a successor. The sages say that it was almost as though Elijah was being recalled to heaven where he belonged, and commanded to find a more down-to-earth man to

---

1 Kings 19:19-21; 2 Kings 2-8 and 13:14-21.

complete his unfinished work among men. The fact is that, after the fateful journey to Mount Horeb, Elijah returned with a mission that he could not carry out to the end. Like Moses, he left this task to his disciple—in this case Elisha, who was more suited to the tasks of anointing a new king of Aram or setting up a new royal dynasty in Israel.

The short description of the initiation of Elisha as a prophet is unusual and may help to explain something of the relationship that existed between Elisha and the other prophets around Elijah. From the textual evidence, it is clear that Elijah was a solitary figure. He appears always as a man alone, eccentric, severe in his judgments of men and events. He was obviously unsuited to the leadership of a band of prophets and could not possibly have bred another Elijah. This was not the result of any basic failing but was in the nature of the man's greatness, there being things that cannot be reproduced in miniature.

It was inevitable therefore that the encounter between Elijah and Elisha should be a meeting of dissimilar types and temperaments. Elisha did not belong to any band of prophets; like Amos, he could say that he was neither a prophet nor the son of a prophet. The role was simply thrust upon him, without previous preparation or training.

In anointing Elisha, Elijah performed one of the greatest of his remarkable miracles, changing a simple peasant, plowing behind a team of twelve yoked oxen, into a prophet, equal to him in stature. The choice of Elisha was, of course, essential for the continuation of Elijah's prophetic mission, precisely because Elisha was, and would always be, to a certain extent, a farmer, bound to things earthly. He remained a practical man, who understood the problems of the common folk, who could grasp the realities of politics, and who could wholeheartedly participate in the pain and privation of the people.

Elijah, in contrast, moved in another world: he belonged in the deepest sense to the mountain of God. He was bound to the fate of the solitary, to the fate of the exceptional individual. Rising heavenward in a chariot of fire was an appropriate end for Elijah.

Elisha remained a man of the soil all his life; as a prophet, he was a glorified simple man. His prophecies lack the majesty and splendor of Elijah's and yet seem to have been more effective.

Elijah was not prepared to compromise in any way—and this is one of the reasons that, despite his repeated demonstration of higher power, he was not politically successful. He was prepared to risk the loss of everything rather than tolerate an equivocal situation: "How long shall ye be between two opinions?" (1 Kings 18:21). He was even willing to imperil the election of Israel at

Carmel, if that would bring about a decision in one direction or another. "If Baal is the true God—then follow him," but do so wholeheartedly.

One cannot really understand the period of Elisha, or even the whole period of the First Temple and the two kingdoms, without paying due attention to the fact that the Kingdom of Israel with all its confused mixture of religious ideas continued to see itself as Jewish. The case of Ahab, who was lured by his wife, Jezebel, into introducing the worship of Baal, was an exceptional phenomenon. Basically, the Kingdom of Israel identified itself as Jewish, and even the cult of the Golden Calf was felt to be a popular form of Jewish worship. Indeed, the Golden Calf of Samaria at Beth El or at Dan was perceived not as a foreign symbol but as something basically and intrinsically "Israelite"—a return to the Golden Calf at Sinai, a legitimate emblem of the essence of Jewish ceremonial. The people of the Kingdom of Israel perceived themselves as reformers, not as an alien, idolatrous cult.

In this context, Elijah struggled not only against the cult of Baal but also against the more prevalent and insidious invasion of religious syncretism, against the development of a form of Judaism that was losing its Jewish content. This syncretism is most vividly delineated in Amos' castigation of the people for their corruption and immorality and for allowing foreign elements to intrude into the ritual. Yet in Amos' day, the shops were closed on Sabbath and Holy Days, even if there was an impious haste to reopen them again. The Kingdom of Israel was still predominantly Jewish, with a more or less observant Jewish population, hardly different from that of the Kingdom of Judah. There was one significant difference, however, and that is the fact that in Israel there was no feeling of Jewish exclusiveness; foreign cult worship was indiscriminately combined with the ancient ritual. Consequently, the struggle of the prophets in Israel, in contrast to those of Judah, was focused not on the nature of the Jewish faith, on the observance of the *mitzvot*, but on the exclusiveness, the purity of that faith.

In this struggle, Elijah was the extreme expression of the demand for an unequivocal breakaway from this domain of corruption. In his refusal to arbitrate either with the kings or with the people, he prophesied complete destruction and annihilation; he doomed them to starvation and death, because he saw things only in terms of black and white. In his own words: "If the Lord be God, follow him; but if Baal, then follow him" (1 Kings 18:21). Between these two extremes, there was no tolerance, no compromise.

Elisha, on the other hand, who was a prophetic force in the reign of Jehu, was very different from his mentor and was prepared to educate gradually, feeling it prudent to reconcile himself to some degree of pragmatism. It was not that he favored compromise or tolerated the existing situation. He certainly had no wish to do anything but uproot the whole spiritual-social structure of the Kingdom of Israel and replace it with another life pattern. He simply chose a different means to this end than had Elijah, who forced the issue by calling for an all-or-nothing decision by the people in a mighty confrontation at Carmel, reminiscent of Moses and the Children of Israel at Sinai. Fire descended from heaven, and the Lord demonstrated that He was God. This confrontation did succeed in temporarily crushing the prophets of Baal; but in the long term, it brought no fundamental change in the social and spiritual climate of the Kingdom of Israel. Even the dramatic proclamation "The Lord, He is God" (1 Kings 18:39) did not shake the people from their old ways. Such is perhaps the case throughout history: the assertion of faith seems to be a real and profound need of communal consciousness; but in daily life, other forces prevail.

Elijah was not prepared to compromise with this hopeless repetition of permanent struggle against the inertia of habit. He justified his zeal during his sojourn in the Wilderness of Horeb: "I have been very jealous* for the Lord God of Hosts" (1 Kings 19:10). This jealousy is to be understood

---

*So the Authorized Version; other versions, "zealous." The Hebrew text can be read in both ways.

as the jealousy of love, in the same way as it is written: "For love is as strong as death; jealousy is cruel as the grave" (Song of Songs 8:6). This incapacity to share one's love is not the same as the grasping desire for the wealth or the power of Baal. It is a need for exclusivity, a need to direct all one's feelings only toward God. Nothing else is possible. So when God asked, "What doest thou here, Elijah?" (1 Kings 19:9), he answered only, "I have been very jealous for the Lord God of Hosts."

This stubborn response was in a certain sense the refrain of his life and the basis of his greatness. It accounts to no small degree for the fact that Elijah, rather than Elisha, became the prophet who caught the imagination of the people for all time. It also explains why Elisha had to be the one to carry on after him.

In the larger historical context, too, it was Elijah who was victorious over the prophets of Baal, and the people of Israel did eventually make the decision in favor of an unequivocal worship of one divinity. As we know, it did not transpire in such a straightforward manner. No single crisis or event, no matter how dramatic, can effect a permanent change in a nation. There was needed an Elisha, with his moderate approach, to accomplish it. True, the religious life never returned to its original purity, as it did in the kingdom of Judah in the Temple; but at least the foreign cults of Tyre and Sidon were eliminated. A fundamental, even if somewhat distorted Judaism was restored to Israel, and Jehu's heirs and descendants came progressively closer to the ideals of Judaism. Furthermore, the biblical account (2 Kings 6) reveals how Elisha came to be more and more a counselor both to the King of Israel and to the King of Judah. He therefore succeeded in gradually effecting changes in the Kingdom, not with a single impressive act or deed but, like the peasant he was, with steady persistence. He plowed, sowed, and waited patiently for his harvest. He knew that he could not achieve dramatic results and that the meager fruits of his labors would have to accumulate in order to become significant. The history of the kingdom was marked not only by the meanness and failure of the sons of Ahab but also by an astonishing resilience. By the reign of Jeroboam II, it had grown again almost to the size of the kingdom of Solomon.

There were other crucial changes, too. Jeroboam II proved by his attitude to the prophet of his reign, Amos, that he was influenced by Elisha, and was able to accept, with understanding if not with equanimity, the words of a prophet who warned of the destruction of his kingdom. The difference between Ahab and Jeroboam II is that, from the reign of Jehu onward, the royal house came under the influence of Elisha. The prophet exploited his miraculous abilities and the power of his visions, not to undermine or even to alter radically, but to effect a change of direction, to bring about the restoration of the kingdom of Israel to its original Jewishness. It is this change of direction that his disciples after him worked hard to achieve.

Elisha and his disciples could not entirely prevent the eventual fall of the kingdom, but they did succeed in accomplishing certain things that Elijah had not succeeded in doing, by virtue of the fact that, unlike Elijah and most other prophets, Elisha was not a "spiritual person." One can hardly characterize him as having the divine madness of an Isaiah or a Jeremiah. Before becoming a man of God, he was a practical, rather composed individual, well in control of himself, and this aspect of his temperament did not change. He was granted the gift of prophecy, but he remained essentially the same man. He probably continued to think of himself as the plowman, the tiller of the soil laboring always for something that would materialize only in the future.

Elisha was not a prophet of indignation and conflict, although he did not withhold his admonitions and rebukes. He was, however, full of understanding of the weaknesses of men and endeavored always to find the most realistic solution in any given situation.

20

Jehu

CALCULATED CRAZINESS

The emergence of Jehu as King of Israel is the rise not only of an individual but of a whole dynasty, perhaps the most successful of those short-lived dynasties that ruled over the hapless Kingdom of Israel from its beginning to its end. Not only did the house of Jehu reign for a relatively long time, but it also boasted some of Samaria's greatest politicomilitary achievements. Jehu's grandson, Jeroboam II, in fact extended the kingdom's borders to almost the size of the realm of David and Solomon, even restoring to some extent the outward splendor of the ancient monarchy. This success was due largely to a combination of political contingencies and historical circumstances that made it possible temporarily to shake off the yoke of Aram. Be that as it may, there

---

2 Kings 9, 10.

is no denying the resilience of the dynasty, especially in periods of crisis and failure.

The biblical account of Jehu consists largely of a description of his anointing and his first acts as king of the Samaritan kingdom of Israel some generations after its secession from Judah. The most dramatic part of the account describes Jehu's seizure of power. We have here an unusually detailed narrative of the event, even more vivid than the report of the rebellion of Jeroboam, son of Nabat, against Rehoboam, Solomon's son, with its factual account of the social and economic background of the uprising. From the Scripture we can understand why the situation was ripe for Jeroboam's rebellion, but we are given little insight into the personalities involved and their personal motivation. How and why was one insurgent rather than another positioned to launch a successful rebellion? It is left to the sages to fill in the gap.

The other successful incidents of rebellion against the Israel monarchy culminating with the establishment of a new dynasty fall into a consistent pattern. A powerful official—usually a military officer—usurps the throne of a weak king. One can assume that a strong king takes steps to avoid a military rebellion. In ancient Rome, for example, it was axiomatic not to allow generals to become too popular. However, during a period of succession when a not particularly powerful or established personality inherited the throne, the situation all but invited a military overthrow.

It was only where sovereignty was legitimized by something other than power that insubordination could be avoided. In the Kingdom of Judah, there were hardly any serious attempts to overthrow the dynasty of David beyond occasional palace intrigues seeking to replace one legitimate heir with another. The position of the house of David as the only rightful ruler of the kingdom was so profoundly embedded in the minds of the people that the intrusion of a usurper, even a charismatic military leader, was unthinkable.

In the Kingdom of Israel, however, military coups were a constant feature of political life and were largely determined by the appearance of "the right man at the right time." Jehu made his appearance at such an apt moment: the house of Ahab had produced only weak and incompetent successors to the throne, and it was evident that someone strong and capable had to take over. The only question was, who?

As mentioned, the biblical account of the insurrection is unusually detailed (2 Kings 9:6–13). Jehu was seated in a public place with some fellow officers when the prophet, a messenger of Elisha's, came in and asked to speak to him. When they were alone, the prophet anointed Jehu with oil as the King of Israel, telling him to "smite the house of Ahab thy master." The prophet then opened the door and fled.

The events that follow on this episode are illuminating not only in regard to Jehu himself but also as an indication of the spiritual state of the country. Jehu's fellow officers asked him, "Wherefore came this mad fellow to thee?" and when, after feebly trying to evade the issue, he told them that his visitor had announced, "Thus saith the Lord. I have anointed thee king over Israel," their response was spontaneous—and unanimous. They snatched up their cloaks and spread them under him, sounded the trumpet, and shouted, "Jehu is king."

A thoughtful appraisal of this scene brings to light the ambivalent relationship of the people, and even the leaders, toward the prophets. On the face of it, it appears that the prophets were without influence on the life of the country and that their moralizing and sermonizing, in Judah as in Israel, had brought almost no dramatic changes: life carried on as it always had; neither social structures nor moral standards had been at all affected by prophetic wrath. Attitudes differed somewhat in the two kingdoms: in Judah, there was great tolerance and respect for the man of God, while in Israel, the response was actual disdain and scorn, and few practiced what was preached to them. Nonetheless, the prophets were, to some extent, objects of awe. People regarded them as perhaps a little mad and their message as irrelevant, and yet as messengers of God, possessed of supernatural powers that can alter the world order. When a prophet preached repentance in the abstract, nobody paid much attention; but when he came with specific tidings, a call to war or to desist from war, to dethrone a king or raise a usurper to the throne, the power of prophecy became very real. In this context, it is possible to understand the sudden switch from ridicule to deadly earnestness on the part of Jehu's officers when they heard the words of the prophet.

King Ahab and his sons had digressed far from the acceptable and the tolerable in their religious comportment, and in introducing the cult of Baal they had somehow brought in an element not only foreign but actually antithetical to Judaism. The fact is that, even if the Jews of Samaria felt a certain guilt or embarrassment about their religious lapses, they nonetheless considered themselves to be Jews, even good Jews, who simply followed the widespread practice, in Judah as well as in Samaria, of paying casual homage to Ashtoret as well.

The foreign cult of Baal, however, associated with Tyre and Sidon, aroused great hatred and animosity, especially against Ahab's queen, Jezebel, its chief protagonist, and this smoldering sense of outrage permeates the biblical narrative. To be

sure, there were surely influential and vocal advo-
cates of Baal, but these did not ultimately represent the true national consensus. Jehu's rebellion
succeeded so well because it represented a genuine stirring of the true spirit of the kingdom, and
also because Jehu was able to harness this deep
resentment against the house of Ahab.

Another factor, to be sure, was Jehu's striking
personality. His wild spontaneity, his craziness,
became apparent from the moment he was declared king by his companions. There is a savage
humor, too, in his driving furiously about in his
chariot, "For in craziness did he drive" (2 Kings
9:20), stirring up the people who came toward
him by saying, "What hast thou to do with peace?
Turn thee behind me" (2 Kings 9:19). He seems
to have conquered the kingdom by the very
strangeness of his behavior.

This element of savage humor is evident also
in his instructions regarding the killing of Jezebel
and the rest of the house of Ahab. His command
that Jezebel be tossed out of the window, and his
letters to the elders of Israel in Samaria demand-
ing the heads of the seventy sons of Ahab, seem
to reveal a taste for the grisly in excess of the *real-
politik* requirements of the day (2 Kings 10:1-2).
What he does is both practical and decisive, yet
there is a strand of "in craziness did he drive" that
is woven throughout.

Even his highly efficient plan to eliminate the

worshipers of Baal is related to his eccentric personality. There are certain theatrical details in the plan, such as his insistence that the worshipers wear special uniforms and expel any outsiders, that bear the fingerprints of Jehu's singular style. But in this case Jehu's plan became the model for innumerable politicians the world over throughout history. Inviting all of one's unsuspecting enemies together for a celebration, only to murder them all in one fell swoop, effectively eliminates the possibility of their resurgence.

How is one to interpret Jehu's singular manner? There is certainly a way of talking, acting, and relating to people that is intrinsic to a person like Jehu, and one can never be sure whether he is joking or deadly serious. Jehu, at all events, was always efficient, even if his actions were carried out with almost farcical "deadpan" indifference. This touch of gruesome humor was more than a personality trait; it is reminiscent of various tyrants who have harbored the need for a defensive deception, a desire to hide the terrible efficiency of their ingenious plotting. Some historical personalities have hidden it by a display of ineptitude or muddleheadedness, while Jehu seems to have used his savage humor as camouflage, as a way of baffling his opponents so that they did not take him seriously until it was too late.

From the biblical narrative, one may gather that Jehu had somehow managed to survive many

years of despotic rule and even to occupy important military posts, such as adjutant to Ahab, precisely because of the apparent eccentricity of his
behavior. Had he been taken more seriously and
perceived as a real threat, he would have been
eliminated by Ahab. Underneath this disguise, he
was able to husband his real strength, climb to the
highest positions, and gain the loyalty of his fellow officers. David once used a similar device to
save his life, when he feigned madness before the
king of Gat. In any case, this tactic of acting crazy
does seem to have protected Jehu from the suspicious eye of the petty tyrants of the house of Ahab.
It enabled him to survive and, eventually, to seize
power at the first real opportunity. It also allowed
him to complete his coup with great speed and
resolution and to establish a new dynasty in Israel.

21

Jezebel

THE GREAT QUEEN

ezebel was, first and foremost, an alien queen. She can be understood only in light of the fact that she was a stranger coming from a world with an outlook radically different from that of the kings of Israel, the good and the bad alike. Jezebel was an outsider, the product of a foreign culture.

Even Ahab, who is certainly numbered among the evil and the sinful who have no place in the hereafter, still maintained many of the forms, and even the laws, of Jewishness. Jezebel, on the other hand, acted in a way that was incompatible with the habits and customs of even the wicked kings of Israel. These kings—good or bad, strong or weak—were usually the products of the instability and rebellion of the country. Nevertheless, all

---

1 Kings 18:31, 21:5-25; 2 Kings 9:30-37.

of them observed, to some degree, the traditional laws of the Jewish people, and their personalities and behavior reflected their Jewishness. Even the kings of Aram knew that the "Kings of Israel are benign monarchs"; and if this benevolence and grace were often politically unwise, their very nature required that they be so, notwithstanding.

In this context, Jezebel was an alien figure whose notions and values were completely different from those of the people around her. The Scriptures are critical of Ahab and condemn him as a sinner who caused others to sin. It was even prophesied that he and his descendants would be destroyed without a trace. Yet, it was also said: "But there was none like unto Ahab, which did sell himself to work wickedness in the sight of the Lord, whom Jezebel his wife stirred up" (1 Kings 21:25). Thus, Ahab was seen as a sinner, but one whose sin was the result of his wife's influence. For as strong a figure as was Ahab, he was dwarfed by the force of Jezebel's personality.

What is more, Jezebel became more powerful after Ahab's death, when formally she had far less right to rule. In a certain sense, she is reminiscent of Catherine de Medici, wife of the French monarch, and mother of several kings who, like the sons of Ahab, came to the throne in succession while their mother manipulated all the intrigues of the royal house from behind the scenes. Like Jezebel, Catherine was, in a way, the reason for the failure and downfall of that particular royal dynasty. She, too, was the most hated woman of her time, but, unlike Jezebel, she died a natural death.

Characteristically, Jezebel did not act for her own sake or in the interests of her father or her former homeland, Sidon. She did what she did in accordance with what she perceived to be the interests of the Kingdom of Israel, trying to strengthen the kingship in general and her husband's position in particular. She was quite unable to understand the uniqueness of Israel where, contrary to the situation prevailing in neighboring lands, the king was a kind of constitutional monarch, his power limited by the law and the formal framework of the judicial authority. No less than this, the kings of Israel were also, to some extent, inhibited by moral feelings. Jezebel epitomizes an alien worldview that sees the king as more than an absolute ruler, as being, more or less, a god. His will was not only law but also the determining morality.

In this sense, Ahab and Jezebel represent the contrast between the Jewish and the non-Jewish world. Ahab was perhaps not a good Jew—he sinned and caused others to sin—but he was still Jewish in terms of his weaknesses, his sensitivity to certain things. Thus, the feeling that the rule of law must prevail, and that he was not merely the overlord of the people but, to some extent, also their servant. Ahab knew that there are limits that must not be overstepped; hence, his behavior over Naboth's vineyard. This is a case where the law of property rights prevailed: the right of a man to retain the estate of his fathers. Ahab could commit the sin of covetousness, could coax, threaten, and, in fact, do his utmost to try to circumvent this law, but it never occurred to him that it could be altogether ignored. And it certainly did not occur to him that the king could unhesitatingly use any means at his disposal to gain his ends. Ahab committed many and various sins, but he sinned in the context of a man with a moral sense.

In contrast, Jezebel was amoral. She was not simply an evil woman, but a woman with no notion of what morality means. She was in harmony with her own world, and she did everything in its interests and to further the well-being of the king. In a certain sense, she was a remarkably good wife; and when she saw her husband downcast because he could not satisfy this or the other caprice (and one that certainly had no national implications), she carried out the most complex maneuvers to satisfy his whim. She built a complicated case for an unfair trial in order to bribe and threaten the elders. She hired false witnesses; she created a complex edifice of deceit, running the danger of compromising all the parties involved, simply in order to fulfill Ahab's ambitions for a particular plot of land. In all of this—in bribing the judge, in conspiring with false witnesses, and in killing Naboth—Jezebel apparently had no stirrings of conscience, while Ahab could not withstand the prophet's curse. In this passage, the difference between the husband and the wife is very sharp: Jezebel remained faithful to her education, to her personality, which was trained for fidelity with no moral strictures beyond the personal tie. She was not even guilty of extreme selfishness but was simply being true to a consistent, pagan idea. She was faithful to her husband, to his country and the dynasty and inheritance of her sons. She did her utmost to uproot and overthrow anything that was likely to stand in their way, or that was deleterious to their well-being.

The fact that Jezebel introduced the worship of Baal into Israel is not necessarily an indication of any religious commitment to that cult; neither is the fact that she consistently acted to destroy God's prophets. Both were simply part of the same phenomenon. Jezebel tried to build a caste of priests and prophets who would be dependent on the ruling house, just as in the other royal courts of the region. She tried to establish a class of intellectuals acceptable to her and economically dependent on the royal house. In fact, during Ahab and Jezebel's reign there seems to have been more support for the prophecy than under any other ruler in Judah or Israel. Jezebel had prophets of

Baal and prophets of Ashtoret and others, who ate at her table, and whose beliefs she was interested in promoting on condition that they be subject to her rule.

It was not religious fanaticism that caused Jezebel to kill the prophets of the Lord. The polytheistic worldview is usually a far from exclusive one; its underlying assumption is always that, since there are many gods, one more or less will not make much difference. Jezebel's complaint against the Jewish prophets was not their insistence on the worship of the one true God, but their lack of "discipline." They had a different system of beliefs and opinions that held, among other things, that the state was not everything, that the king was not a god, and that he could be told hard, plain truths. It was this that Jezebel could not, would not tolerate at any stage in her political life, in any way, shape, or form.

Even after Elijah had confronted the prophets of Baal on Mount Carmel, and it seemed that the whole nation, including the king, seemed intent upon renewing the relationship with God, at least temporarily, only Jezebel did not respond. Instead, she immediately threatened Elijah with death for killing the prophets of Baal. Her goals were simple ones. She was dedicated to a limited number of things that she thought must be done, and one of them was immediate compliance with the desires of the king. Any obstacle to the fulfillment of the royal will could be dealt with only by annihilation.

Jezebel's sons (rather weak and apparently unable to act of their own volition) ruled under her protection and with her backing as the great queen. Even those who looked askance at Ahab's royal line knew that the power rested not with Ahab, or with his sons—small people, transient and inconsequential—but with Jezebel. Although officially she was only the dowager queen—a position of honor but no power—Jezebel transcended this role: she asked for reports of what was happening and for assessments of what was going to be. Most interesting of all is the description of her last moments, of her meeting with Jehu—himself a hard, strong man—only moments before he sent her to her death. This meeting proves, among other things, that Jezebel was, in fact, the real ruler of the country at the time. Her personality was revealed in all its force at the moment of her downfall. Even then, when she knew that the revolt had been successful, that she no longer had any cover, any protection, she maintained her equanimity, insulting and belittling Jehu. She knew that she was exposed, totally vulnerable, and about to be killed. Despite this, or perhaps because of it, she took care to appear at her best and adorned herself as if for a feast. In the face of imminent death, she used her knowledge of the history of her adopted country to insult the new king. She pleaded neither for compassion nor for mercy but merely demonstrated her scorn of Jehu. She comported herself like a queen to the end.

It is interesting, too, that even Jehu responded to Jezebel in a special way. He revealed a great deal of contempt toward the house of Ahab and his offspring, treating the children as if they were vermin. He suggested with characteristically savage humor that the nobles of the country either wage war against him or else bring him the heads of Ahab's sons. The only person for whom Jehu evinced some little respect was Jezebel, and he gave the order to bury her remains because, as he said, "She is a king's daughter" (2 Kings 9:34). Even those who hate Jezebel see her as extraordinary, not as an object of scorn or ridicule. Despite the repugnance and hatred she generates, they perceive her as a thoroughly royal figure. At the same time, there is the feeling that Jezebel was a source of evil, a root of abomination within the Kingdom of Israel. It is she who first gave official status to an alien rite, who interfered with the rule of law, and who introduced alien political norms into the nation. The assessment of Jezebel is that she was an evil woman who dwarfed those around her.

We do not know whether Jezebel was beautiful or ugly, whether she was intelligent, or anything else about her as a person. Certain traits in her personality are so strong that all her other characteristics are blurred. Almost all we know of her is that she had enormous willpower and self-confidence. The sages regarded Jezebel as corrupt but as an integrated personality—not a "patchwork" figure. Measured against her, Ahab, one of the most wicked kings of Israel, appears insecure and hesitant.

If Jezebel had other faults and private vices—as may be inferred, albeit with some reservation, from the phrase, "the whoredoms of . . . Jezebel and her witchcrafts [that] are so many" (2 Kings 9:22)—they did not conflict with or impair the central focus of her life. She is perhaps the most perfect representation of the force of evil in the whole of Scripture. Her whole being was focused on will, and she was a bottomless well of aggression and strength, single-mindedly convinced of the justice of her acts. She saw herself not only as a queen but as the epitome, the realization, of the Kingdom of Israel, not a "mother in Israel" but a "queen in Israel"; and in a certain sense, she tried to give a new image to that monarchy. She wished to give the country a new character and to tear out the roots of inhibition and restraint that stood in her way—the belief in God, the prophets. Thus, she said to Ahab, "Dost thou now govern the Kingdom of Israel?" (1 Kings 21:7). She tried to build a new state, based on new principles that she believed to be healthy, normal, and sound; and she attempted to educate the whole nation accordingly. Those around her, even those she loved or respected, must act according to her instructions, not because she wanted them to be subservient to herself but because she wanted to build something new, a new ideal, of absolute monarchy. This ideal appeared to the prophets and in the Scriptures as the essence of evil.

In the history of other nations, women like Jezebel have created the exemplary image of the "great queen" or at least the figure of the queen whom history calls great. Catherine the Great in Russia, who also possessed colossal willpower, and Queen Elizabeth I of England were admired by other nations. In Israel, however, although Jezebel was respected (because no one would deny she was a great woman), the attitude was different. The prophets fought hard against this kind of personality, even while they appreciated and were impressed by its greatness. They measured it against a different scale of values and, since they did not concur with the way of temporal power, rejected Jezebel, seeing in her the personification of evil.

22

Athaliah

THE LUST TO RULE

Queen Athaliah is one of those historical figures who leave a great impression despite the lack of factual material about them. To be precise, her only direct quotation consists of two words; all the rest of our information is but a truncated list of her deeds and acts at various times. Nonetheless, the little that we do know creates such a fascinating picture that it is not surprising that Athaliah has become the subject of several plays, some of them quite well known.*

Athaliah's known biography is very simple and can be told in a few sentences. She was the daughter of Ahab and married Joram, King of Judah. After he died, their son Ahaziah took his place. This king of Judah, who was the grandson of King

---

2 Kings 11.
*Most famous is the play by Racine (1691).

Jehosaphat, had friendly ties with the Kingdom of Israel and with the house of Ahab. But when Ahab's house itself was overthrown by the coup of Jehu, the wholesale destruction of Ahab's descendants and family included Ahaziah, King of Judah, the son of Athaliah. Athaliah then took an astonishing step and did away with all the royal family (among them perhaps her own descendants) and herself assumed the reins of government. She was the sole ruler of Judah until, in the end, a conspiracy was formed against her and the throne was returned to the child Joash, son of Ahaziah. Athaliah was killed, and this strange wave of palace intrigue disappeared from Jewish history.

The first point that should be mentioned here is the political aspect. Athaliah was the first woman to hold real power over the whole Kingdom of Judah. A later queen, Shlomzion, at the time of the Hasmoneans, earned a reputation and great esteem for herself; and other women have ruled the nation or at least held high political positions. However, it is the first precedent that deserves special mention, and that precedent is Athaliah. The surprising thing is not only her ability to take the government upon herself but also the considerable length of time during which she actively ruled over the people and the kingdom.

The destruction of the royal line—and, apparently having no apprehensions regarding the

women, she was careful to destroy only the males—
eliminated all potential claimants to the kingship.
But, in fact, by killing off the male line, she also
destroyed whatever legitimate claims she may have
had to remain on the throne. In the absence of
hard scriptural evidence, we can only wonder
about the circumstances that allowed a woman
with no legitimate claim to hold sway over a nation totally unaccustomed to female rulers. And
we can only speculate about her personal motivation: What drove this woman and at what was
she driving?

The scanty material available leaves a great deal
of room for speculation regarding not only Athaliah's inner motives but also the internal political
structures of the Kingdom of Judah. Although she
was the first woman ruler of the kingdom, there
had been many previous instances of queens ruling in the East. Not all of these queens ruled in a
completely legitimate fashion, since their right to
rule was not completely supported by law; but
their governments were no less strong or less
stable than those of their male counterparts. The
outstanding example is Queen Hatshepsut, for
many years the acting ruler of Egypt, who shows
that even within a culture where the monarch was
outstandingly a male figure, a queen could reign
and take upon herself (with few exceptions) all
the titles of kingship. It is known that the statutes
of Hatshepsut depict her as a man, with a mag-

nificent beard, expressing the idea that she (as was said of another woman) was regarded as "the only man in the government."

The fact that Hatshepsut could reign for an exceptionally long time over a large kingdom with an ancient tradition of kingship shows that there were certain politicohistorical precedents of women rising to power, and that the problem of the legitimacy of their rule did not, apparently, present an insurmountable obstacle. The conditions necessary—indeed, imperative—for a queen to maintain power were: a stable royal succession, not shaken by frequent rebellions; and a cultural tradition supporting the power held by a reigning sovereign, against whose rule there was no appeal. These conditions, which were true for the Egyptian Queen Hatshepsut, were also true for queens of other lands, all over the world. We simply have no example of a woman establishing a dynasty or of a woman ruling over a state that is politically or militarily unstable. Only in a state with a high degree of political stability can we find a woman who is not only the formal holder of the crown, but also the actual ruler. This situation is clearly attested by the annals of European royalty —England, Russia, Spain—where a queen's rule could be based only on a tradition in which orders were transmitted through established channels, and people did not inquire too closely into the nature of those orders or the qualities of the individuals who issued them. Queen Athaliah's rule was possible under specific conditions like these and then only because she ruled in the Kingdom of Judah, where a single dynasty had reigned for many years, and where there had not been a single real revolt or serious attempt to overthrow the royal dynasty. Thus, Athaliah, who in fact had no real claim or right to rule, could, in the absence of other claimants to power, govern the state for six years— a fairly long period. In the Kingdom of Israel, on the other hand, there would have been no possibility of a woman retaining power for any length of time. In that unstable state, even the legitimate kings were fairly likely to be toppled by others.

There is another aspect to Athaliah's "case." If she had come to power a few years earlier, it would have been claimed that the queen was getting political help and support from the members of the ruling house of Israel, to whom she was related. The surprising thing is that Athaliah took up the reigns of government after her family and her power base in the Kingdom of Israel were destroyed to the last man. At such a time, there should have been a popular response against foreign rule (it should be remembered that Athaliah may have been Jezebel's daughter and, in any case, was not from Judah but from Israel and was thus, from every viewpoint, a foreign transplant).

Nevertheless, despite all these strikes against her, Athaliah maintained control of the government for a considerable length of time. Her removal from power was the result of a conspiracy in the highest circles of the kingdom, and not as the result of a popular revolt. There is no doubt that Athaliah lacked real supporters among the masses of the nation or the army. Nevertheless, the latter were prepared to accept her rule for many years without expressing any marked opposition. This fact indicates that Athaliah had wielded unusual power in the state during the reign of both her husband and her son and did so not merely as the result of her formal position. Even in the days when there was formally some kind of king, it became clear that everyone involved knew who the actual ruler, the real "boss," of the country was. The person who made the decisions was the dowager queen, the king's wife, the queen mother. Thus, even when the legitimate holder of the government disappeared, his ministers and clerks continued to accept this woman's authority. The impression is that, over many years, they had grown accustomed to receiving from her the crucial instructions, the policy decisions. Only in this way is it possible to explain the subservience to her commands, some of which should certainly have aroused opposition and disgust. Thus, Athaliah's rule can be explained by the general political stability of the Kingdom of Judah and her fiercely aggressive personality.

A more serious problem is that of Athaliah's

motivation. Although there is no unequivocal way to explain the phenomenon, it appears that there were here, among others, two interconnecting factors, even though they do not in themselves provide a complete answer to the question. On the one hand, it is clear that Athaliah, like Jezebel, was not just a strong personality but a woman who yearned to rule—a woman with a real ambition, an intense passion for power. To rule was for her not merely a means of attaining some desired objective and certainly not an opportunity to indulge in the benefits of wealth, influence, or the magnificence of royalty. Her passion was simply for power itself, and this drive of hers was so strong that it caused her to carry out a series of extreme acts, even to the point of destroying the royal heirs. The strange and inexplicable element in all this is: Why did Athaliah destroy the royal progeny?

From subsequent events, it turns out that at least one child remained alive, the boy who later became King Jehoash. It seems that Athaliah's son did not die childless but left some offspring, including daughters, some of whom were left alive. Jehoash was actually saved by a sister of the previous king, Jehoram, Athaliah's husband. We may assume that Yehosheba, Ahaziah's sister, was not Athaliah's daughter but the child of another woman. At all events, there were other children, and Athaliah did not try to safeguard them, not even the baby grandson in order to be able to rule as regent in his stead. Instead, she tried totally to destroy the children of the royal house in order to acquire full control and power without fear of any contenders to her throne and with no need to hide behind someone else. Another woman who acted in a similar way, although not to the same extent, was the last ruling empress of China, who was known as the "dowager empress." She did not take upon herself all the formal trappings of government but, in one way and another, over a period of many years, destroyed all the people who were the formally designated rulers of the state. During this time, she reigned unopposed, eliminating anyone, including her own offspring, who posed a threat to her power.

Athaliah's personal feeling of loss, her lack of all normal social and family ties, seems to have fed a different drive. As long as her son was alive, she remained somehow within the human sphere, not only because he was the rightful king, but also because of her emotional contact with the child. She hungered for power and probably wielded real power, but she did not yet need all its external trappings. The downfall and destruction of her father's house was the event that broke Athaliah's last ties with the rest of humanity. What remained was simply this one drive: the lust to rule, apparently not linked to any specific political goal. That is to say, Athaliah did not try to establish a new royal dynasty; she did not try to transfer her authority to anyone coming after her. She did not even make any serious political or religious changes within the country. She became simply a manifestation of this one drive: to rule. It seems as if all human restraints and inhibitions, all feeling, vanished from her psyche. Without the slightest concern for the future, she built herself a totalitarian government, of limited legitimacy, bearing only the stamp of her own personality. In her attempts to destroy the house of David, she seems to have been acting out of a wish to bury the whole world, to draw the whole country into her tragedy and suffering, and to fulfill the only remaining emotion left to her: the lust for power. She would be the last ruler, seeking to survive not because of any higher goals, but as the final expression of a personality in its death throes. Her sons, with the exception of Ahaziah, were killed by enemies; the house of her father and brother and family, the whole house of Ahab, was destroyed in Israel; and the last link with any kind of life, with any kind of responsibility for her actions, collapsed. She had set out to destroy the world—an urge that was not self-destructive, since all that remained of her was the insane will to rule. Athaliah sank into the intoxication of the lust for power. She was a woman alone with no future and no past, stripped of human ties and devoid of emotions, leaving her only with her demented ambition.

23

Josiah

THE LAST MONARCH

There is no limit to historical speculation, even though most attempts to figure out "what would have happened if . . ." are usually fruitless. The number of possibilities is often so great that speculation becomes mere guesswork. There are a few instances, however, where we can allow ourselves to say with conviction that had not this or the other person been killed before his time, the course of events would have been significantly different.

Toward the end of the First Temple period, there was at least one such personality in Judah. King Josiah's life and tragic death changed the face of the kingdom and probably had a profound effect on the development of the nation as a whole.

2 Kings 22-23; 2 Chronicles 34-35.

Although the biblical text itself provides relatively more information about Josiah than about most of the other kings of the age, there are still many gaps in the account. In any event, we know that the discovery of a lost Book of Moses was a decisive factor behind Josiah's actions; other factors can only be surmised.

No matter whether the actual book discovered was one of the five books of Moses or a commentary on some prophetic work, what matters here is what Josiah did with it. He took it with the utmost seriousness and used it as the foundation for restructuring the whole social and religious fabric of the nation. In this sense alone, Josiah exerted a significant influence on the life of the people for many generations—an influence that was greater than can be measured by the events following on the discovery of the book. It is written of Josiah: "And like unto him was there no king before him, that turned to the Lord with all his heart, and with all his soul, and with all his might, according to all the Torah of Moses; neither after him arose there any like him" (2 Kings 23:25). Even the prophet Ezekiel, no admirer of the royal house, held Josiah in esteem, as did Jeremiah. In these sources, as also in the Book of Chronicles, Josiah is seen as the last hope of the nation in its own land because he was the last great monarch of the Kingdom of Judah.

Josiah's death, which was an accident of war or

politics, not only caused a series of crises concerning his heirs but also brought about—at one stroke—the irreparable destruction of all that he had tried to build. After the death of King Josiah, the fall of the kingdom and of the First Temple became inevitable, only a question of time. After him, there was no one who could withstand the threat of foreign influence, on the one hand, and the vast pressure of internal problems, on the other. If the fall of Judah was delayed after Josiah's death, it was only the result of larger political circumstances; it could no longer be averted altogether.

The prophet Ezekiel referred to Josiah thus: "Moreover, take thou up a lamentation for the princes of Israel. And say, what is thy mother? A lioness" (Ezekiel 19:1-2), contrasting him to the other unsuccessful "whelps" whom she had brought into the world. Jeremiah, who certainly knew the king personally and may be assumed to have been closer to him and in sympathy with him, is spoken of as lamenting his death (2 Chronicles 35:25). There is an established tradition that the fourth chapter in the Book of Lamentations, beginning "How is the gold become dim," is the expression of Jeremiah's grief at Josiah's death. The verse "The breath of our nostrils, the anointed of the Lord, was taken in their pits" (4:20) has come to symbolize the profound sense of loss at Josiah's passing. It is unusual for a prophet to speak so highly of a king. A king of the Jews is, to be sure, the anointed of God; but a prophet's calling him "the breath of our nostrils" seems to indicate that Josiah's fall must mean the fall of the kingdom. The coming destruction was not yet apparent at the time of his death, but Jeremiah as a prophet must have known that it would come.

Josiah, as a man, stands far above the other kings of Judah. Jewish historiography has attributed only one failing to him, and that was an excessive enthusiasm, as when he attempted to prevent Nechoh, the Egyptian pharaoh, from marching through his land. We have no reliable information concerning the reasons for this battle in the vale of Megiddo, a battle that for all its excellent strategy seems to have been foredoomed by the military might of the Egyptians. Perhaps the fact that he did delay Pharaoh and weakened his fighting strength may have tipped the balance of the great battle of Carcemish, as a result of which victory Babylon, under Nebuchadnezzar, achieved complete control over the civilized world of the period, for at least seventy years. In any case, this was the only serious error attributed to Josiah; and the sages explain it by saying that he was trying to forestall the plunder of the country and that, thus, his intentions were noble, if misguided. It was an error based on a profound love for the Land and the people: he was prepared to risk his own life to prevent despoliation and waste by an invader. As against this single mistake, King Josiah's achievements were indeed formidable. There are kings whose historic greatness rests on internal reforms, and others whose efforts go to strengthening the country against external forces. Josiah worked on both fronts, but since his efforts never came to fruition, they were never recognized for what they were and were not clearly reported in the written history of the times. Neither the Book of Kings nor the straightforward biblical Chronicles do more than hint at Josiah's achievements, but it is from these hints that we can reconstruct something of his remarkable endeavors.

It may be appropriate here to recall the nature of the political situation in Judah and in the region as a whole at the time. The power of Assyria had been in decline for some years. The last king of Assyria, as we now know, was something of an amateur archeologist and left behind one of the largest and most interesting libraries ever discovered in the ancient world. As a king, he seems not to have made an impact on history; while his empire tottered, he engaged in archeological digs and was generally to be found elsewhere than where he was supposed to be. The political forces that took over from him did not exert much power on the area around Judah, and a political vacuum was created in the region that had formerly been the Kingdom of Israel. Josiah persistently strove to annex those territories whose former inhabitants (known to history as the Ten Lost Tribes of Israel) had been banished, and which, nominally at least, were counted as one of the provinces of the Assyrian empire. Josiah did not go about this annexation by any demonstrative political or military act, but rather inconspicuously, by putting the territory under his personal jurisdiction. No doubt he was one of these people for whom action precedes words and who do not bother to explain their plans and intentions to anyone.

It appears that Josiah acted slowly and with persistence in a way that may have been calculated to fulfill the words of prophets uttered many years earlier. He went to Beth-el and burned bones on the altar there, perhaps the bones of Jeroboam, son of Nebat. This symbolic act of burning the remains of one who had departed from the path of the Torah—and, what is more, to do it on the altar of the Golden Calf at Beth-el—was of profound significance. It was a public declaration that the old rebellion against the kingdom had been illegitimate, and that the memory of that first rebel was now purged. At the same time, it was a defilement of the altar that may be said to have symbolized the revolt of the Kingdom of Israel against Judah. Thus, by his action at Beth-el, Josiah proclaimed the nullification of the Kingdom of Israel as an independent force and declared his intention of restoring the united kingdom of the days of David and Solomon.

The fact that Josiah could even consider going forth to battle at Megiddo, the very heartland of the former Kingdom of Israel, seems to point to the fact that his control of this territory was undisputed. It was not Josiah who had declared himself the king of all the lands "unto Mevo Hamat," but he did apparently try gradually to draw together all the remnants of the people of the Kingdom of Israel. He sent messengers to gather in the exiles and attempted to restore the allegiance of the surviving remnant to the cult at the Holy Temple in Jerusalem.

It is evident even from the scanty material available that the process of unification did not take place all at once, nor was it done without a certain amount of coercion. The picture that emerges is that, with a most unusual firmness and consistency, Josiah sought to restore the magnificence of the kingdom of David and Solomon. He had a vision and never doubted the importance or value of his own endeavors to bring it to realization.

Therefore, Josiah's achievements cannot be confined to the discovery of the lost volume of the Scriptures and its aftermath. The publicity that he gave to the harsh prophecies against the Kingdom of Judah and its monarchs points not only to his piety but also to his political courage. He exploited the most appalling prophecies for the constructive purpose for which they were meant, using them to give a new face to the kingdom. True, others before him had attempted to restore the central worship at the Holy Temple in Jerusalem and to force the elimination of the various "high places" all over the country; but in spite of coercive measures, these attempts had not been successful.

Josiah tried to get the people to share and cooperate in his religious enthusiasm. He did not want to manipulate a revolution from above but preferred to lead a popular revival based on mass support. It was in this respect that Josiah used the prophecy of Jeremiah and of Huldah to build a broad popular base for their common goal: a spiritual revolution that would transform the people's relationship to God. This goal was only accomplished generations later after the destruction of the Temple.

For generations, the prophets had delivered the warning that the Holy Temple and the kingdom itself were not necessarily eternal, that the country might collapse about them and the people be sent into exile. The nation did not seem to absorb the meaning of this terrible message; it never became clear to them, even after the Israelite kingdom of Samaria had been destroyed. Josiah was the first king to endeavor to learn the lesson of the fall of the sister kingdom, and he became convinced that no small nation like Israel or Judah could stand up to the great powers of the world unless it was resolute and inwardly integrated.

This was perhaps the guiding principle in his long-range political dream for Judah. His aim was to restore the kingdom to its former size in the days of David. Beginning with the nucleus of the two remaining tribes of Judah and Benjamin, he sought slowly to build up a military and political force with his own loyal supporters in key positions. Like David, he encouraged prophets to come to him and to be a permanent part of his court; he wanted the men of God to be his friends and not his enemies.

Josiah furthers his broad program with typical imagination and breadth coupled with pragmatic gradualism. He patterns himself on King David's strategy: He begins with a small nucleus, in this case, Judah and Benjamin, and, with the help of trusted friends and the military, attempts to slowly expand into a large kingdom. Like David, who, despite their chastisement, looked to the prophets Nathan and Gad for direction and support, Josiah embraces the prophets of his day. Josiah is a true scion of David; his is a messianic attempt to restore the splendor of Israel to its rightful place.

The meaning of what Josiah was trying to accomplish was apparent to those who could grasp its scope; hence, the terrible shock felt by the prophets at his untimely death, when he was not yet forty. Had he, like David, lived another thirty years or so, he might have succeeded in restoring at least some of the splendor of the days of his illustrious forebear. His death in battle was one of those tragic quirks of history in which accident suddenly cuts off all chance for the carrying out of some vital project. No one rose in his place—no one with his political acumen or sincerity, no one with the ability to fulfill his grand designs.

At Josiah's death, Jeremiah lamented for the Jews' last chance, their last chance for many generations. His expression of grief at the loss of "the breath of our nostrils, the anointed of God" was also an outcry of deep pain by one who may have seen with the eyes of a prophet the route that the entire history of the Jewish nation was to follow: exile, humiliation, and decline; and only after many generations, to rise again and be renewed.

24

Ezra

THE IDEOLOGICAL LEADER

he period that opens the Second Temple era is fairly well documented. There are still many gaps in our knowledge, as there are in all the accounts of ancient times, but we are given far more information regarding the first fifty years or so of this period than for the two hundred years following.

Such documentation as we have regarding the beginning of the Second Temple era is to be found in the books of Ezra and Nehemiah, which are fairly straightforward accounts, and in the later prophets: Haggai, Zechariah, and Malachi. These biblical chronicles present such a clear picture of the historical processes of the period that one is able to separate and define three separate waves of immigration and reconstruction.

Book of Ezra; Book of Nehemiah.

The first wave of immigration was that immediately following the proclamation of Cyrus, King of Persia, permitting the Jews to return to Jerusalem. This group of immigrants was led by Sheshbazzar, a prince of Judah, probably one of King Yoachin's progeny; by Joshua, the high priest; and by Zerubbabel, son of Shealtiel. We have no idea of the exact relations between these men, and it would prove valuable if we could somehow probe them. Be that as it may, the fact is that this was a first *aliyah*, a wave of immigration to the Land of Israel. We have many details of this first *aliyah*, such as the number of holy vessels, even the number of pack animals brought by the immigrants (Ezra 2:66-67), and the way they began to rebuild the destroyed Temple (2-3) and Jerusalem.

The new immigrants suffered many vicissitudes as a result both of internal problems and disputes and also of external pressures. These pressures were not the product of any well-defined political design. The neighboring peoples were themselves not yet national entities; they were rather ethnic groups or communities—some of quite ancient origin, like the Ammonites, others just beginning to take shape, like the Samaritans. All seem to have resented the intrusion of the returning Jews who were clearly out to reestablish their own state, while the problems of the new Jewish community were made even more difficult by the fact that they themselves were far from being a single ethnic group.

Yet another problematic factor was the imperial policies of the central government in Persia that were subject to frequent changes. The biblical account records its contradictory instructions: to build the Temple, not to build the Temple. This mixed message inevitably had a disturbing effect on the newly established community; and, according to the evidence of the later prophets Haggai, Zechariah, and Malachi, it was in every way a period of considerable instability and uncertainty.

The second wave of immigration was smaller than the first but carried considerably more weight. Led by Ezra, the scribe, this group, composed of idealists and intellectuals, was more conscious of its task, better equipped, and backed by the central government. Thus it could function without the restrictions that applied to a Jewish province within an imperial administration.

The third wave of *aliyah* followed not many years later with Nehemiah. This group was also small, mostly workers and military men, and had the personal support of the king so that it was able to settle certain acute problems of the new community.

These three waves of immigration formed the basis for the resettlement of the Land, although there was a continuous influx for many generations thereafter. They established the fundamental pattern of life in the times of the Second Temple, and all that followed was a variation on a more or less fixed theme.

To further characterize these three waves, the "first" *aliyah* was led by Sheshbazzar, by Joshua, the high priest, and by Zerubbabel, with the spiritual guidance of the prophets Haggai, Zechariah, and Malachi. Haggai and Zechariah are mentioned several times in the Book of Ezra, but Malachi is a more obscure figure whose name may have been no more than a sobriquet. In any case, it is certain that the first immigrants were full of naïve enthusiasm: they felt they were returning home. Most of them had a specific connection with the Land, whether it was to ancestral estates or to hereditary tasks in the Holy Temple. The pioneers clearly had no idea of the problems awaiting them and were probably overwhelmed by the sheer magnitude of the unanticipated difficulties. At the same time, the support they had expected to receive from their brethren in the country and outside was not forthcoming to any significant degree. They were thus immediately confronted by oppressive economic difficulties, because of both inadequate planning and general bungling as well as a lack of work and money. Moreover, the repeated occupation of the Land by neighboring peoples, although it never reached a stage of open warfare, was an everpresent source of anxiety and tension.

The functionaries of the central government, even though they remained officially neutral, were also unfriendly. The immigrants' task clearly demanded considerable labor and patience, but their response to the situation was generally ambivalent. On the one hand, there was a genuine feeling of joy at being able to realize the hope of rebuilding the cities and the destroyed Temple. On the other hand, there were many voices raised in complaint and protest about the wretched way things were being done. Confusion and sadness seem to have been the lot of these first settlers, and they often needed to be spurred on and encouraged by their leaders. The spirit of ambivalence that characterized the period is captured by the description of the new Temple's dedication: along with the shouts of joy at the rededication could be heard the sounds of weeping for how pathetically it compared to its predecessor.

In many ways, the arrival of Nehemiah was crucial. Not only was he a man of great spiritual and intellectual powers, but he was also a brilliant man of action. True, his spiritual ideas did not show any real originality, but he knew how to get things done.

In contrast, Ezra, the scribe and priest, came to the country armed with considerable formal powers from the king and with a great deal of political assistance, but was not able to cope with the practical difficulties that faced him. An officially signed letter from the king was enormously effective in the Persian empire—as we also know from the Book of Esther. A document of this kind gave Ezra the authority to do whatever he wished in order to restore the ritual at the Temple in Jerusalem; he also enjoyed economic support from the government and wide powers to punish—by fine, flogging, or death—anyone who did not comply with his wishes. Yet it seems that Ezra, either by circumstance or by choice, preferred to achieve his goals by other means.

Nehemiah, on the other hand, who came with much less clearly defined official sanction, was possessed of keen political knowledge and understanding. He had been personally close to the king and, if necessary, could approach him over the heads of all the officials and governors. Even if he lacked Ezra's legal authority, Nehemiah knew how to maneuver tactically. He used his small private army with efficiency and decisiveness.

One of the situations recounted in the Bible that rather neatly delineates the contrast between the two leaders is their reaction to intermarriage with, and participation in the abominable practices of, Canaanites, Hittites, Ammonites, and other local peoples. When Ezra learned of the "offense of these exiles," he said, "I rent my garment and my mantle, and plucked off the hair of my head and of my beard, and sat down appalled" (Ezra 9:3). Nehemiah learned of it in another context and hoping to improve their political and religious lot. The saga of the ship *Mayflower*, with its significance for the whole later development of the United States, is only one example. What is interesting is the similarity of the problems of peoples who migrated with such an urge, and the way they formed clusters of settlement unified by commitment to definite ideological concepts. The only difference is that the *aliyah* of Ezra preceded similar movements by about two thousand years.

On the same basis, one may view the covenant of Nehemiah (Nehemiah 9-10) as the first constitution in history. Composed in accordance with his political and religious policy, it is the archetype of the modern legal constitution pertaining in most states: that is, it contains a lengthy preamble presenting the history of the nation, its origins, and its aspirations (in this case, to restore statehood in accordance with the spirit of Judaism), followed by a detailed listing of basic laws, ordinances, and regulations required to give the covenant executive power. In addition to the Torah, which was defined as the accepted basic law, there was a sequence of social and economic legislation appropriate to the time and, only thereafter, a list of important persons setting their seals in the name of the people. Among the signers were representatives of the large families and recognized leaders like Ezra and Nehemiah. By setting their seals to what was called the *amanah*, the "covenant," they pledged themselves to the first written constitution in history, the beginning of the modern concept of law as a mutual agreement among free men.

It may therefore be inferred that Ezra endeavored to accomplish something unprecedented. He and his companions strove for something that went beyond the physical restitution of the state. Coming as Ezra the priest and scribe charged with the task of reinstituting the Law of the Torah in the Land, he saw himself as a teacher and guide, an ideological leader. This ideological factor was indeed paramount in all his actions and complemented his singular personality. When the king offered to provide him with a private guard, he refused on the grounds that, as a person who claimed to receive divine help, he felt it would be ridiculous to rely on a body of soldiers for protection—and this in spite of the fact that he had good reason to be frightened.

Ezra was quite aware of the need for other methods besides the ideologically inspired ones. He knew he could not force a value system upon the unwilling. Consequently, he tried to bring people to the desired point of acceptance of their own free will. This inevitably led to difficulties and opposition from all directions; and, at least at the first stage, not everything that he attempted showed results.

Although the people of his *aliyah* almost certainly agreed with Ezra's politicoreligious approach, and although he had brought with him a large contingent of Levites and others intended to be teachers of the Torah, there was no denying the fact that most of the Jews in the country had become tired and apathetic. He realized that he would have to change this situation, and not by official decree alone but by persuasion and by personal example—by spiritual action as well as by teaching.

Ezra therefore called for fasts and for public demonstrations of solidarity and penitence. He felt that the coercive powers vested in him by virtue of his royal powers were not suited to his aim. He wished to bring about an ideological transformation in the people. This was a change that required time, and it took many years for some of Ezra's statutes to become an intrinsic part of the life of the Land. Tradition has it that Ezra instituted ten ordinances, each one of them intended to introduce spiritual force and outlook into existing social and political values, great and small.

Nehemiah was the practical man of action, but it was Ezra who was undoubtedly the one who laid the grand pattern of restoration. By giving new content to old forms, Ezra's achievement was such that the sages said: if the Torah had not been given by Moses it would have to have been given by Ezra. In a sense, the achievement of Ezra is parallel to that of Moses: while Ezra did not mold the people into a nation, he did, nonetheless, effect in them a profound transformation. The Jews ceased to be a rather ordinary political entity and became a people who expressed and manifested the spirit of Torah. It may be said that the Torah was received again through Ezra, less dramatically than on Sinai, but no less significantly for all that.

25

Esther

A MISSION IN THE HAREM

he Scroll of Esther is an intriguing and astonishing instance of a miracle that has no supernatural element whatsoever. It has no trace of a *deus ex machina* or of mysterious happenings over and above the events, which themselves radically change the situation. Rather, all the motivations, desires, and explanations are plain to be seen. In principle, this is an important key to understanding the significance of the Jewish attitude to miracles. It is clear, at least insofar as something of this nature can be clear, that in Jewish thought the essence of the miracle is not identical with the supernatural event but is linked to its significance, its content—and its result, arising from the combination of forces and personalities involved.

Book of Esther.

Thus, in the Scroll of Esther, where everything is apparently revealed and comprehensible, the narrative is in a certain sense misleading. When we examine the details of the story, it becomes apparent that this is a complex tale, with several levels of which only the edges are visible. Deeper penetration reveals different aspects of Esther's role and even of her being. From the moment of her being taken to the palace, we discover an interesting and instructive phenomenon in regard not only to the sequence of events thereafter but also to their significance.

The fact that Esther had come to live within the palace was not planned: that is to say, she was not an emissary of Israel sent to operate within the king's house. Nor was she the prototype of the beautiful spy planted in the courts of the enemy. However, from that moment, even before she became queen, it is clear that Mordecai had ideas of his own, and that ulterior thoughts of his directed Esther's steps. Both Mordecai and Esther were fully aware of the possible importance of her being in the royal house; and thus, from the outset, there was a certain readiness for appropriate action that ultimately bore fruit.

At the time when Esther first came to the harem, neither she nor Mordecai knew what lay ahead. Haman's deeds and influence, his rise to power, were not yet apparent and, indeed, came only later. It is very likely that, in the early stages of

Esther's sojourn there, neither his enmity nor his anti-Jewish programs had taken shape. However, Esther was preparing herself for, or at least showing an almost inspired awareness of, what could happen in the future—as is attested by the fact that initially she "had not shewed her people nor her kindred" (Esther 2:10). This discretion was not simply accidental, nor was it necessarily a case of self-interest. Rather, Esther was acting here on the express instructions of Mordecai to whom, as is explicitly stated, she was still obedient (2:20).

There is here no attempt to hide from anti-Semitism in the modern sense. It was very likely that King Ahasuerus, like most Persian rulers, was more or less tolerant of the religions and peoples in his domain. Yet Esther was introduced into the palace in such a way that it was not at all clear to which nation she belonged—an uncertainty that was the first indication of what was to follow. In everything that Esther was to do there was an element of surprise. It is interesting that Haman, himself an interested party, did not discover Esther's Jewishness until after he was powerless to do anything about it; and since he did not know of her origins, it did not occur to him to act against her.

Therefore, the first stage in Esther's becoming the king's favorite did not bring advantages to "Mordecai's people"—as the Jews are referred to in the book. It was common in those times for the women of the harem, the favorite concubines who reached a senior position, to be rewarded with a series of benefits and privileges for members of their nation. In almost every culture with a similar social structure that we know of, foreign concubines acted in the interests of their own compatriots or members of their own faith. It was apparently so in the court of the Mongol khans and in the Turkish empire, to give but two instances. In some cases, like China and Japan, preferential conditions for the queen's relatives were a permanent and influential factor in internal politics. There are many instances all through history of the influence of the favorite queen or concubine being of great historical importance.

The fact that Esther, in accordance with Mordecai's instructions, did not overtly seek such "fringe benefits" proves that we have here a case of inspired foresight or, at the very least, an awareness of "the sorrow that is to come." There is here an implicit realization of the fact that a representative within the king's court could be more useful if her Jewish identity were not recognized. In the context of modern-day espionage, Esther is a "mole," a person who over the long term infiltrates the system, working in the best interests of the system in which she is planted, so that at a crucial time she can be activated for an important mission.

Esther is an almost classic example of the conspiratorial connection. On the one hand, she did not disclose "her people or her kindred," even though the king tried various means to extract the secret from her. She actually appeared to be an orphan, someone without relatives, in a way that was somewhat damaging to her status. For, after all, someone without connection, background, or roots was inferior. In the long term, this inferior status appeared preferable to the premature disclosure of her origins. In addition to this "secrecy," Esther and Mordecai were in almost daily communication, whether directly or by means of messengers bringing reports to and fro between them. These reports were probably not always important, although at other times, they may have been crucial. The single instance recounted in the book concerns a different kind of communication. This is the incident in which Mordecai used Esther in order to forestall a rebellion that was being plotted against the king. Here, too, Mordecai's action went beyond the immediate issue at hand: he had reasons of his own for preserving the connection with Ahasuerus, who seemed to him more "amenable" than other likely candidates to the throne, if only because of his relationship with Esther. Hence, it seems likely that the Esther-Mordecai relationship went beyond the regular family bond, and that Esther was in fact carrying out a mission, whether knowingly and voluntarily or whether in response to her uncle's commands as instructor and guide. Esther was the unacknowledged emissary of the Jews within the palace. It may be that, from the outset, Mordecai was simply using her to learn about what was going on in the country generally, but it is also likely that he was farsightedly thinking of possible future developments.

In truth, it was Mordecai who "engineered" the high point of the drama: the moment in which Esther revealed herself as a Jewess and reached the zenith of her political achievements by overthrowing the most important man in the country—Haman. Mordecai not only guided Esther's steps but also encouraged her and spurred her on. He showed her that the crucial moment had come to act, even if that act incurred grave danger to her position and, if the king were so minded, even to her life. This was the moment when she must fulfill her task, regardless of the cost to herself.

It is interesting that another aspect appears at this point, which, even if only hinted at in the Bible, seems to be of profound significance: that is the power of prayer at a crucial moment. Mordecai's prayer is mentioned in the Septuagint—not in the original, but it is still evident from the context.

Esther's feeling that she had come to carry out a great task, her commitment to her people, and her belief in the Jewish way of life and values were evident when she asked Mordecai to call for a three-day fast to pray for the success of her mission—in memory of which, the Fast of Esther is observed to this day. Esther's request reveals not only the strength of her bond with the people but also reveals the extent of her faith in the efficacy of the prayers of the Jewish people and her feeling that she represented their spirit within the palace.

An understanding of Esther's deep commitment to her people changes any initial impression we may have received of her as a woman who, if she did not sell her honor, at least compromised it by going complacently to the palace, losing contact with her past, and becoming a woman of the harem. Here, her role was to be pleasing in the sight of the king, to amuse and satisfy him—with all that this role implies. Yet there are other hints of Esther's true character—some very fine and faint, others very clear.

There is the danger she underwent for the sake of the nation, and her declaration that a day of celebration and feasting be initiated to commemorate the events. This was the act of a woman who had carried out a dangerous mission and felt a need to perpetuate that mission, not only in the deepest social and national sense but also as something of profound significance in her own life. She felt her deed had value as a sacrifice and epitomized the many tasks fulfilled for national or ideological reasons.

Into this category must come those tasks, difficult and perhaps among the less pleasant, that women must sometimes carry out to achieve their goal: to surrender themselves totally, while protecting their identity and remembering where loyalty must lie. It is not an easy temptation to withstand. In the case of Esther, she was not involved in a dubious or temporary love affair but actually became the queen, reaching the heights of ambition and achievement that a woman in those days could perhaps hope for. Nevertheless, Esther felt that her task was more important, and that it was up to her to represent the Jewish people at this moment. When Mordecai confronted her with the choice between her mission or her rank, her status, and—not least—her life, he was making things very difficult for her. On the one hand, Esther had attained the highest possible position, that of queen of an empire, and she was likely to lose it at one stroke. On the other hand, if she betrayed her mission, she would be a traitor to all the values and beliefs that sustained her in her years at the palace.

The sages have evaluated a role of this kind in connection with both Yael and Esther: "Greater a transgression for the sake of heaven than a good deed which is not." This saying, dangerous to those who abuse it, expresses an understanding of the spiritual dedication that goes beyond mere personal danger and involves also a degree of personal humiliation, a renunciation of self. From the point of view of the Jewish woman, Esther's role was not honorable. Had she married a fellow Jew and become a decent housewife in the capital or elsewhere, the feeling would have been that she was fulfilling a *mitzvah* (for the sake of heaven or otherwise) in a perfect, dutiful way. The very fact that she was in the palace to begin with was, in a certain sense, the result of a chain of "transgressions in the name of God." Midrashic and talmudic literature expands this notion and penetrates deep into the problem of this total devotion. The moment when Esther was required to go to Ahasuerus, and use every means of seduction and temptation at her disposal in order to lift the sentence of death that had fallen on the Jews, was not just a moment of personal danger. She was required to pass from a passive state to an active one, to become the temptress. Previously Esther could claim that, to some extent, she was in a situation in which she was held under duress. From the moment when she took the initiative in approaching the king to seduce him, she lost her last shreds of innocence. Where previously she could feel pure, at least in spirit, she was now to some extent sullied. The step Esther took in approaching Ahasuerus with a view to enthralling him by her personal charm was a step more drastic than her induction into the king's harem, a matter in which she had no choice. Consciously, she now decided to endanger not only her life but her soul; and from this moment onward, she becomes the savior of the Jewish people. Inwardly, however, she could no longer regard herself as belonging to the ethical values of her people, not in body and perhaps also not in soul.

Other generations have maintained that, when a man gives up his life while his soul is pure and unsullied, he has reached one level of sacrifice, and that there is a further level, where an individual not only gives up his life but also exposes his soul to a danger whose result none can foretell. This test of sacrifice, the hidden, unexplained test that is not stressed in the Scroll of Esther, changes this woman from a mere historical figure to a national heroine. The mechanism of the miracle is plainly revealed and visible. All its elements are clearly spread before us. Esther is the woman around whom this miracle revolves, the savior whom we later bless in the religious festival of Purim recalling her act of heroism.

26

The Woman of the Book of Probverbs

RULING FROM THE INNER CHAMBER

t first glance, the Bible appears to be a book dominated by male figures. When we think of biblical heroes, the individuals who come to mind are almost invariably men: patriarchs, kings, and prophets. The women appear as ancillary figures: the wife of this man or the sister of that one. Even a glance at the names mentioned in the Bible will show that while many hundreds of men are listed, there is only a very short list of women's names, ostensibly reflecting their minor role.

This superficial view is misleading. A more careful reading of the biblical stories—even the ones in which women appear to play only a cameo role—will reveal that the role played by women was infinitely greater than is apparent in the scriptural narrative. Their profound influence on events and society is only partially revealed; for the most part it is hidden away between the folds of the Bible passages.

The best generalization of the role of women in the Bible can be found in Psalm 45:14 (possibly a wedding song): "The whole glory of the king's daughter is inward." Biblical woman's cycle of life was veiled, hidden, home-centered. She is separated from the outside world by a curtain, but in terms of life *within* that curtain her status is entirely different. Every woman, not just the wife or daughter of a real king, is a queen in her home, and like all royalty she is sometimes despotic and sometimes enlightened, depending upon circumstance and predilection. The domineering "Jewish mother" is not necessarily a modern phenomenon; it can be traced to ancient times.

An analysis of many biblical episodes, some of them of seminal importance, reveals the decisive feminine hand. Many a man's fate was determined, for better or worse, by the woman in his life, at times by pressure or by seduction or by threat, and at times through sheer force of personality.

One sphere of influence is that which is bestowed upon women by their motherhood. The Early Prophets provide us with two detailed descriptions of mothers decisively influencing their sons. One of them is Hannah, the wife of Elkanah, the mother of Samuel. Hannah craves a child, prays for a child, and by her vow determines her son's entire fate—sanctified to the worship of the Lord, at the sanctuary in Shiloh. Samuel is not merely Hannah's son; he is her creation. To be sure, she could not determine that her son would ultimately be a prophet and judge, but she certainly established that the thrust of his life would be in that direction.

Another mother, of different temperament but of similar influence on her son, is the wife of Manoah, mother of Samson. The sages observed that throughout the story "Manoah went after his wife" (Judges 13:11) and that it was she who was the dominant figure and her husband a mere shadow. She received and applied the prophecy, determined the future, created a new reality. And yet the Bible never reveals her name! This dominant personality, the central figure in the story, is known only as "Manoah's wife." No mere accident, it is a purposeful illustration of the hidden place of the woman, playing a decisive role, yet operating behind a curtain with little, if any, public identity.

This maternal influence may be surmised from the scriptural descriptions of the various kings of

Judea. To each king's name is invariably attached the name of his mother. It has been suggested that it is the personality of the mother that determines that of the king. The differences we encounter between certain kings and their offspring successors are astonishing. There are the pious who succeeded wicked fathers and the pious kings who begat wicked sons. There are unlikely pairs like Ahaz and Hezekiah, Jotham and Uzziah; Manasseh the epitome of the evil king—and his father Hezekiah, who is a Messiah-like figure; the righteous Josiah and his father, Amon. Apparently, within the uninterrupted dynasty, the determining variable was the identity of the mother, and it was she who imprinted personality and character, values and attitudes upon the son. And all this is expressed laconically by the Scripture with the words "and his mother's name was. . . ."

In the examples given, the mother determines the fate of the son—sometimes even before he is born—not through public action but by establishing his path or influencing his direction at a critical juncture. Similarly, other women have engineered a fateful reorientation in the lives of the men they encounter. Abigail cleverly dissuades David from the action he is about to take; she placates him and sends him in an entirely different direction. Later, David is beholden to Abigail for deterring him from bloodletting, a gratitude that leads to their marriage. In fact, the sages have noted that in her initial encounter with David, in which she pleads for the life of her husband, Abigail has already laid the groundwork for their future relationship. "When the Lord bestows upon you all the good He hath spoken . . . thou shalt remember thy handmaid" (1 Samuel 25:30-31). David may have believed that he was the initiator but, in fact, he was being guided by a woman, fortunately a good woman. Similarly, the manner in which Bathsheba arranges for the succession of the throne for her son, Solomon, is an indication of her decisive influence upon David at particularly crucial moments.

This pattern of action can be observed in almost all the female biblical characters, whether they are women mentioned in passing or whether they are major personalities. The relationship between Abraham and Sarah is fascinating in the way Abraham acquiesces each time Sarah takes a strong stand. The same is true of Rebekah; at the critical moment when Isaac is about to settle the matter of the birthright, the woman successfully interferes in favor of her choice.

This gap between the apparent powerlessness of women and their real potency can be found throughout Scripture, that is, although official power was traditionally in the hands of men, ultimate control was largely in women. The king's daughter was consigned to the inner chambers, and from the chambers she always ruled. And she ruled in this manner generation after generation. Indeed, the dialectic between conspicuous male power and hidden feminine power is one of the central characteristics of Jewish life over a very long period.

The examples that we have of women exercising their subtle efficacy are rarely cases of petty desires and personal needs. Usually the intervention extends far beyond personal or family issues in the narrow sense and at times involves matters of great import. Even in property cases where women successfully intervened, the issue was not merely the distribution of family assets and held far-reaching significance. This is evident in the small episode of Achsah, the daughter of Caleb, who successfully forces her father to cede to her husband an important addition to his homestead. So too, the famous five daughters of Zelophehad, whom the sages describe as wise, insistent, and eloquent, were not merely interested in personal gain; their demand had ramifications for the entire tribe. Here again we have examples of women whose names we barely know, exercising their inner strength in a similar way. Continuity in the broad sense is their charge, and they usually take the initiative only when decisions involving basic principles and other matters of far-reaching importance are at stake. All of these elements generalized and abstracted are extolled in the song of praise to the Woman of Valor.

"The Woman of Valor," with which the Book of Proverbs ends, is no simple woman of the house. As many of the verses indicate, she is the house. She does not merely produce garments for the gratification of her husband. As is told in an almost offhanded manner, "She considers a field and she acquires it" (Proverbs 31:16). To be sure, while she is the one who determines how to expand the family estate, and indeed to arrange for its financing, she does it in her husband's name. It is her husband who "sits among the nation's Elders" (31:23).

Another passage in this song of praise has ramifications for all of Scripture: "Grace is deceitful and beauty is vain; but a woman who fears the Lord, she shall be praised" (31:30). Throughout the Bible, a striking aspect of the description of important female personalities—both good women and those not particularly so—is that they are depicted as beautiful. The Matriarchs are almost invariably depicted as being "beautiful and well favored" or "very fair to look upon" or both, and these attributes appear time and again as part of the feminine ideal. Clearly, neither King Solomon nor the Wisdom literature, Ecclesiastes and Proverbs included, intends to denigrate human beauty and to exalt ugliness.

Rather, alongside the power of the beauty that is the Beloved, so graphically described in the Song of Songs, and the power of beauty that seduces, entraps, and beguiles, as described in Proverbs and elsewhere, woman has another inner element that is the ultimate source of her power and influence throughout the Bible.

Unlike other societies—particularly those that are male-dominated, as biblical society largely is—women are not considered to be mere playthings, esthetic ornaments. While ostensibly, physical beauty seems to be an ideal as well as the basis for their power, the essential attitude toward the value and ultimately the power of beauty is that it is in reality transitory, the essential definition of "falsehood" and "vanity" in the Woman of Valor passage. The real source of power is the strength of character that lies behind the "pretty face."

The Book of Proverbs is essentially a compendium of practical advice, although it occasionally rises to theological heights presenting the greater components of the cosmos and of creation. But since the book is essentially very practical, it provides much pragmatic advice and aphorisms concerning a large variety of women. However, as in the Books of the Prophets, the woman of Proverbs is also a symbol of something broader. The sages long ago observed that the Book of Proverbs comprises a mixture of the practical and the sublime and that it is difficult to delineate where the description of the real woman ends and that of the abstract Woman as the symbol of Wisdom begins. To what extent is this glorification of Wisdom as the power that builds and creates the world allegorical and to what extent does it also apply to physical womankind? Similarly, the image of the treacherous and licentious evil woman often takes on a broader dimension when it merges with the concept of specious, traitorous knowledge, evil wisdom.

The final chapter of Proverbs provides an idealization of woman not only as the bedrock of the family, but in the broadest sense, as the driving force behind events. She is the foundation, the basis, from which much else emanates. And this abstraction finds expression in all biblical women, from Eve through Esther. Dominant without appearing to master, they quietly maneuver the men, and their intercession is decisive. If they be like "the Lord-fearing woman who is to be praised," they will alter the course of things in one direction. If they are not God-fearing, their influence will be in another direction. In either case, so much is contingent upon woman in this manifest world in which she barely manifests herself.

Index

Shlomzion, 214
Sidon, 192, 199, 205
Sin
  of Ahab, 204, 205, 206
  Golden Calf and, 96
  of Israel, 102
  of Saul, 161-163
  Tree of Knowledge and, 8,
    99
Sinai, God/man relationship
  and, 7
Sisera, 116, 118, 119
Sister role
  Miriam and, 93-94
  Sarah and, 22-23
Slavery, Joseph and, 76
Social factors
  Abraham and, 16-17
  Baal and, 199-200
  biblical narrative and, xi-
    xii
  conversion and, 143-144
  Elisha and, 188-189, 191-
    192
  harem and, 247-248
  idolatry and, 149-150
  immigration and, 234-
    235
  Jehu and, 196-197
  Jezebel and, 207-208
  Josiah and, 224, 230
  judges, 123-125

Leah and, 61-62
prophecy and, 128-130
Samuel and, 146-151
women and, 141-142
Solomon, 175-184, 196,
  228, 229, 261
  downfall of, 183-184
  foreign affairs and, 181
  personality of, 175-178
  political factors and,
    175, 178-180
  Torah and, 182
  wisdom of, 178-179
Soul, monotheism and, 14
Spiritual decline, Judges and,
  148-149

Tamar, 69
Taxation, Solomon and, 175
Temple, Solomon and,
  182
Temptation, Joseph and,
  69-70
Temptress role, Eve and,
  6-7, 8
Time, biblical narrative and,
  xii-xiii
Torah
  Ezra and, 243
  God/man relationship
    and, 7
  Joshua and, 104

About the Author

Adin Steinsaltz, internationally regarded as one of the leading rabbis of this century, is head of the Israel Institute for Talmudic Publications. In addition to his monumental translation of and commentary on the Babylonian Talmud, Rabbi Steinsaltz is the author of several works in English. His series of discourses on chasidic thought contains *The Sustaining Utterance*, *The Long Shorter Way*, and *In the Beginning*. Some of his other English works include *The Strife of the Spirit*, *The Essential Talmud*, *The Thirteen Petalled Rose*, and *The Tales of Rabbi Nachman of Bratslav*. Rabbi Steinsaltz was born and resides in Jerusalem.